CRAFTING THE SUCCESSFUL BUSINESS PLAN

CRAFTING THE SUCCESSFUL BUSINESS PLAN

by Erik Hyypia
and the editors of
Income Opportunities

PRENTICE HALL
Englewood Cliffs, New Jersey 07632

Prentice-Hall International (UK) Limited, *London*
Prentice-Hall of Australia Pty. Limited, *Sidney*
Prentice-Hall Canada, Inc., *Toronto*
Prentice-Hall Hispanoamericana, S.A., *Mexico*
Prentice-Hall of India Private Limited, *New Delhi*
Prentice-Hall of Japan, Inc., *Tokyo*
Simon & Schuster Asia Pte. Ltd., *Singapore*
Editora Prentice-Hall do Brasil, Ltda., *Rio de Janeiro*

© 1992 by
Prentice-Hall, Inc.
Englewood Cliffs, NJ

10 9 8 7 6 5 4 3

Library of Congress Cataloging-in-Publication Data
Hyypia, Erik.
  Crafting the successful business plan / by Erik Hyypia
and the editors of Income opportunities.
    p.   cm.
  Includes index.
  ISBN 0-13-158924-5
  1. Small business—Management. 2. New business enterprises—Management. 3. Entrepreneurship. 4. Planning.
I. Income opportunities (New York, N.Y.) II. Title
HD62.7.H99 1992
658.4'012—dc20   92-10472
                                           CIP

0-13-158924-5

PRENTICE HALL
Professional Publishing
Englewood Cliffs, NJ 07632

Simon & Schuster. A Paramount Communications Company

Printed in the United States of America

ABOUT THIS BOOK

Every ship's navigator plots his or her course using a map of the coastline showing reefs, currents, and safe channels. Your business plan will be your guide through the rocky waters of start-up onto the profitable high seas of a successful business. It will help you obtain loans, smoothly start operations, and later, even sell your company.

This book was compiled and edited by the editors and staff of *INCOME OPPORTUNITIES* magazine, one of the most respected publications of its kind. Over thirty years of experience and research have gone into the making of this book to help make it, perhaps, one of the most valuable books you have ever purchased.

There is no doubt that you could have learned all that is contained in this book from your own research. But how long would it have taken you . . . weeks? Months? And how much would it have cost you in time and materials? Far more than the price of this book.

It is better that you direct your time and energy toward the establishment and growth of your new business. This book takes you step-by-step through every phase of creating your business plan, and then using it to start your business and keep it running smoothly and profitably.

ACKNOWLEDGMENTS

The Publisher would like to gratefully acknowledge the contributions of the following writers and editors: Erik Hyypia, Arthur Blougouras, Jannean Bryant, and Stephen Wagner, editor-in-chief.

HOW TO USE THIS BOOK

The step-by-step format of this book is designed to make it as simple as possible for you to create a business plan with which to start your own new business. It is our intention to eliminate or minimize much of the doubt, confusion, and guesswork that is often involved in any business start-up.

Before you actually begin acting on Step One, we suggest that you read through the entire manual to get an overall view of the business plan, how you will create it, what it encompasses, and how you will use it. In this way, you will obtain a good basic idea of the work required, the advantages, and the drawbacks — all before you make your first move.

After reading the book through, think about it for a day or two and then, perhaps, read it again. Then you can turn to Step One and begin the foundation of your own business.

It is not mandatory that you follow each step exactly as the editors have presented them here; they are meant as guides to help you find the easiest, quickest route to success.

CONTENTS

INTRODUCTION

WHY HAVE A BUSINESS PLAN?

$\mathbf{P}$aperwork? Like most new entrepreneurs, you probably want to start your own business or take over an existing one. You probably have thousands of ideas and details in your head, and you are itching to roll up your sleeves and get started. Great! However, the idea of starting off with paperwork probably doesn't thrill you.

This business plan you are about to create is your first step in turning your dreams into profitable reality. It is also your most important step. It is the single best way to organize all those details, to obtain loans, and to implement all your good ideas.

Let's suppose that you want to build a boat and make your fortune trading goods up and down the coast. Your goal is reasonable, and since others have achieved it you probably can succeed as well.

But where will you get the money to build your boat? How big will it be? What materials do you need? Where will you find experienced carpenters? Once you launch your boat, can you spot the reefs and shoals? Are there good and bad sailing seasons? Can you patch your boat if you hit a rock? What goods will you carry? Who will buy them? Can you make a profit? What other traders will you compete against? And are pirates waiting around the next headland?

These are some of the tough questions which every new business owner must face. If you answer them before you lay down your hard-earned cash, you stand a good chance of succeeding. If you don't, the odds will be against you.

This is where your business plan comes in. It is a tool with which you examine the details critical to your success. It helps you think about your products and services, your competition, financing, and how you will structure your organization before you make any investments in equipment, buildings or, employees. By planning early, you can avoid the expensive and dangerous maneuver of changing horses in mid-stream.

The business plan helps you get start-up money. Banks and other lending institutions are much more likely to loan money to an entrepreneur with a well thought-out and professionally documented plan than to a person who has scratched his notes on a napkin.

During start-up, it helps you get a handle on all the myriad of details which you will have to face in a short time. And as you ease from the frenetic activity leading up to opening day into daily operations, it provides you with a checklist of milestones which you need to tackle next.

Finally, if the time comes when you want to sell your business and move on, the business plan will be vital to the new owners. With the plan in hand they know what they are getting, and they can be assured that they can run the business at least as well as you have.

Let's take a closer look at what a business plan contains and how you can use it profitably.

WHAT A BUSINESS PLAN CONTAINS

Since the business plan is a multi-purpose tool which helps you plan, finance, start, run, and possibly sell your business, it is composed of a number of different sections. Let's look at each part briefly now.

Don't be intimidated by the diversity of sections or by the business terms used. While the business plans of major corporations can stretch to hundreds of pages in length, many entrepreneurs' plans can be as short as ten pages. Most average about forty pages in length. The rest of this manual will guide you step-by-step through the easy process of writing your own professional business plan, and then using it to build your idea into a profitable business.

The length of each of the following sections will vary with your particular type of business. For example, a "widget-making" factory's business plan might contain a very detailed production section, while the plan for a pizza-delivery business would have a relatively simple production section. You will tailor the length of each section of your plan to your own business needs.

Executive Summary: A brief summary of the current state of the company, what products or services it offers, its markets, its competition, and its finances. This is a quick overview of everything to introduce the company to your readers, which will be the bank or your partners.

Table of Contents: Helps readers navigate through your business plan.

The Company: The objectives, goals, direction, organization, number of employees, facilities, history, key players, tasks, people, flow, overall organization, management, communications, feedback loops, viability, and profits of the company.

Products and Services: Products and services to be sold, what marketplace needs they fill, and standards for quality, quantity, and timing.

Production and Operations: Raw materials needed, sources of materials, processing needed to turn raw materials into finished product, equipment needed, location, buildings, employee jobs, hours, shifts, and subcontracted tasks.

Marketing: The niche the product or service fills, who the consumers are, the scope of market, state of market, and marketing strategy.

Sales: Ordering, delivery, payment, returns, repairs, warranties, guarantees, liability.

Competition: Your competitors, their products, production, niches, marketing, and your advantages over them in each area. (Very important section!)

Risks: The major hurdles facing your company, including financial, competitive, market and other potential problems. Lets you anticipate and fix problems before they happen.

Finances: Costs of start-up, production, marketing, and sales. Profits, budgeting, financing needed, sources of financing, financial plan.

Milestones: A time-line of major events and of hurdles to overcome during the start-up and growth of your business. This acts as a checklist of tasks for you to accomplish.

PRE-PLANNING: BEFORE YOU LAY DOWN YOUR MONEY

You will probably find money in short supply for a while, as do most entrepreneurs starting their own business. It is therefore vital not to waste your precious cash. As with romances, beginnings are fragile times. When you write your business plan, several very important things will happen.

First, you will be taking a hard look at every aspect of your business before you invest your hard-earned cash. You can easily change strategies, investigate new markets, and change the nature of your product on paper, all for no cost. The business plan supplies you with these necessary questions you should be asking at this time.

Second, the decisions which you will be making will determine the course of your business for years to come. The time to make these decisions is now. Why? Imagine that you are building a house. If you lay the foundation and start framing, only to find that you need another room, you will have to rip down some of the walls you have just sweated over, wasting valuable time and money. If you wait even longer before you discover that you need another room, you might have to tear the roof off, rip up interior paneling, and ruin carpeting as well! Big decisions are cheap when made up front. The later they are made, the more expensive they become.

Third, many new businesses fail because they lack adequate start-up capital. You will need enough money to obtain a building, equipment, raw materials, or inventory. You will need to pay salaries (including you own) for the dry weeks or months before customer's checks start rolling in. And you will need a cash buffer in case equipment breaks, you get sick or some other disaster hits at a crucial time. The business plan gives you a means for determining just how much money you will need to safely get through your start-up period.

Fourth, unless you are financially well-off, you will probably need to obtain a loan. Banks and other lenders are much more likely to give you a loan if you can show them a well thought-out business plan. Enthusiasm is great, but you will need to use your business plan to back it up with solid facts. Your plan will give them the realistic information they need to approve your loan.

START-UP: THE CRITICAL FIRST TWO YEARS

Your plan will help you in several ways as you begin to implement your new business. You will be faced with a hectic period of weeks or months as you gather equipment, people and materials, and put the show on the road. First, using the "equipment" section of your plan, you have a checklist of items to buy, rent, or lease. By carefully examining this list, you can determine which items are vital immediately, and which expenses you can put off until later. Then, list in hand, you can comparison-shop for the best prices.

Second, the "employees" section of the plan will help you advertise for employees and effectively screen the people who respond. By using the criteria you lay out in your plan, you can determine which people best match your job openings. You can also use the job descriptions to accurately inform each potential employee of what his or her duties and responsibilities are to be.

Third, the "training" section of the plan will help you quickly bring new employees "up to speed" in their particular job. Fast and efficient training avoids wasted time, damaging mistakes, and other problems.

Fourth, the "finances" section will provide you with a measuring stick to determine how well (or badly) your business is doing against expectations. By examining true costs against the costs you have detailed in the plan, you can identify problem areas and take corrective action early. Remember, the first rule in making money is not to lose money.

Fifth, your investors or financial sponsors will want to see how well your business is measuring up to expectations before they fork over more money for additional loans. By comparing your books against the plan, you have an important "reality-check" which you can use to both show them how well you are doing, and to show them that you are identifying trouble spots and taking corrective action.

Sixth, the plan provides milestones to measure your progress. These important indicators show you (and your investors) if you are progressing, or if you have stagnated at a particular stage, or even worse, if the business is back-sliding.

MATURING: GROWTH AND EXPANSION

Once your new business is established and the profits are rolling in, you may decide that it's time to expand. Expansion that is planned and executed logically usually leads to more profits. Haphazard expansion riddled with decisions which are not carefully planned can flush a company's finances down the drain.

Once again, the business plan is the key. By using the existing plan as a base, you can identify which areas of your business can be expanded, how much work it will take, and how much profit or loss each type of expansion will bring. Then you can make a sound decision on where to re-invest your profits. Since you already have a living, breathing plan, you don't have to start from scratch. You merely have to modify certain areas of the plan.

As with the start-up phase, the modified business plan is also useful for obtaining additional financing, facilitating the details of the expansion, and monitoring progress.

MOVING ON: SELLING YOUR BUSINESS

The day may come when you want to sell your business. Perhaps you want a new challenge, or see a better opportunity. Or maybe you want to retire. Or, the business may be on the rocks. Your up-to-date business plan is a vital ingredient in the sale. When a potential buyer looks at your business, he will be searching for several things.

Has the business been profitable? Obviously your business will be more saleable if it has been making money for you. He will need to examine goals, milestones, and costs and profits contained in your business plan and in your account books to prove this point.

Is it running smoothly? What are the day-to-day operations like? Are employees happy, do materials flow into the business smoothly, and are quality products produced reliably? Your "products," "production," and "organization" sections help answer these questions to the satisfaction of the potential buyer. Are plans in place which will keep the business running smoothly when it is turned over to the buyer? When a new owner takes over a business, his employees often know more about it than he does. The staff will have to run almost autonomously for a while until the new owner becomes fully versed in the operational details. The up-to-date business plan can greatly facilitate bringing the new owner up to speed and make this unstable period of autonomy easier for the employees to bear. This minimizes the shake-up of the employees, new owner, and customers alike.

Can customers be assured of a healthy change of ownership? The business plan reassures important clients and lending institutions of the continuing viability of the business, and prevents panic pull-outs and the resulting loss of sales and support.

The well-maintained business plan facilitates a smooth, well-oiled, and profitable transfer of ownership.

TIPS ON WRITING YOUR BUSINESS PLAN

1. Skim this book: Your first task, right now, is to quickly skim each chapter and get a feel for what each section contains and why it is needed. Skimming does two important things. It gives you an overview of the complete business plan you will soon write, and it starts your creative juices flowing. Questions and ideas about your own new business will begin filling your mind.

2. Write your own business plan: Next, open this book to Step One and take your pencil in hand. Read the Examples section of the chapter, thinking about your own business ideas. Then follow the straightforward how-to steps to write your own. Write your notes on the worksheet page at the end of each chapter. Don't worry about spelling or neatness or format now. Just get your ideas down on paper.

    Hint: If you get stuck with writer's block, describe your business to a friend (or to the mirror) verbally. Most people are much more comfortable speaking than writing, and will find it easier to "talk it out." You can even talk to your tape recorder, then later transcribe your relevant thoughts onto paper. This really works! Try it.

3. Take a break: Once you have completed all the worksheets and have written your "rough draft," put this book and your notes away for a few days.

Go have some fun. Let your brain cool. This is a secret all professional writers use — by getting away from the work for a little while, you can come back to it with a clearer head. Defects which need polishing leap out, omissions become obvious, and unnecessary and unimportant words are easy to spot and clean up.

4. Write your final draft: This is the easy part. Open this book to Step Nine: Create Your Final Business Plan, and follow the instructions. You will take those rough worksheets and polish them up into a professional document which you can show to any banker, potential partner, or employee.

5. Print the final copy. You're almost done. Take your final draft to a professional word processing service. Almost every town has some sort of business store or copy center with a computer word processing service. They will type your final draft into the computer, create the bold "headers" and graphics, check your spelling, and print out the final document on a laser printer. The results are quite impressive.

6. Use your business plan: The remaining steps show you how to use your business plan to get money, how to navigate through your start-up year, how to run day-to-day operations, and should you ever want change of pace, how to sell your business.

Remember, this business plan is your first step to creating the new business you have dreamed about. You now have the chance to be both the dreamer and the realist, the artist and the architect. Sure, it's a lot of work — but you can do it!

Step One

CREATE A "PRODUCTS/SERVICES" SECTION

WHAT YOU WILL SELL

This section of your business plan describes what you will sell. You might sell physical items such as food or clothing; you might sell a service, such as television repair or car washing; or you might sell both products and services.

Since the product (or service) is at the heart of your business, it pays to take time and examine all the details now. Many products or services are relatively simple and straightforward, as in the case of a self-service laundromat. Other products need more description, as with a convenience store which sells a large variety of magazines, auto and personal supplies, food, drinks, snacks, and so on.

Whatever your product might be, you will need to tell your lenders what you are offering.

CONTENTS OF "PRODUCTS/SERVICES"

Products: This is a list or description of the physical items which you will offer, what they are and what they do. It includes core items (your main sales items), peripheral items (extras), and if these items are for sale, lease or rent.

Services: This section describes your core services. For example, if you are starting an auto repair shop, your core services might include repairs, adjustments, routine servicing, and inspections. It also clarifies what you do not offer (body work, painting, cleaning). It describes your peripheral services, such as warranties, guarantees, servicing, delivery, or after-installation adjustment and inspection.

A Need: All successful businesses share at least two things in common. They offer some product or service to a market, and there is a need in the market for that product or service. Without a need, no one will buy a product — no matter how good it is.

Changes: You might be working to change the product line in the future. New market conditions, availability of supplies, and other factors might require you to adapt your products in some way. This description of anticipated changes helps you plan for the future needs before they become critical.

EXAMPLES

[Example # 1]

CONTINENTAL CUISINE CATERING

Catering is an increasingly lucrative business in Longmont, Colorado. The white-collar population is rapidly increasing due to an influx of new high-tech corporations in the area, and this well-to-do population has repeatedly shown its affinity for elegant, prepared social events.

Continental Cuisine caters a variety of European cuisines including French, Italian, and German breakfasts, lunches, and dinners. The menus include options for full bar ser-

vices, salad and soup smorgasbords, dessert bars, and elegant coffee services.

Entrees can be cooked on-site in full view of customers, providing visual value as well as excellent meals. Desserts and other non-entrees may be prepared before the event at the Continental Cuisine kitchens and delivered to the event.

Continental Cuisine is a full-service caterer which provides a full range of supplies and services as well as food, leaving the host free to enjoy his event. We supply everything from tables and chairs to elegant fresh floral centerpieces and even musical entertainment. Our staff does all set-up, cooking, serving; break-down and cleanup of the event; and books and manages entertainment.

[Example # 2]

THE SURF CAR WASH

The Surf Car Wash provides a variety of automatic and hand automobile cleaning services. Customers can first gas-up at the fuel pumps, then use self-service coin-operated vacuums to clean their interior. Next, a computerized "brushless" drive-through tunnel provides fully automatic exterior and undercarriage cleaning and waxing, with several cost and service level options. Mitt men at the exit of the tunnel buff the car dry and clean interior windows and dashes. This automatic service fills the needs of most of the commuter population on heavily traveled Federal Boulevard, where the service is located.

Some automobile owners require a higher level of meticulous detail in the care of their machines. The Surf also offers a comprehensive hand-detailing service. Surf employees hand-clean windows, vacuum and dust the interior, and steam-clean carpets. Then after a careful exterior cleaning, wax is hand-applied, and the vehicle's chrome is polished. Other options include tar removal, leather treatment, waterproofing of fabrics, paint deoxidization, wheel repainting, and engine steam-cleaning.

In the customer waiting area, The Surf sells auto accessories such as ice scrapers, window cleaning fluid, floor mats, drink holders, and cassette tapes. All of these items are frequently requested by a large segment of the driving population. Vending machines provide drinks, candy and snacks to waiting car owners.

Though The Surf does not currently do any engine or other mechanical work, we are planning to add an oil-change and inspection bay to the operation in approximately two years. This will allow customers to accomplish all their routine servicing with one easy stop.

HOW TO WRITE YOUR OWN "PRODUCTS/SERVICES" SECTION

1. Products: What Physical Things Will You Offer?

List or describe your main products. If you build three models of vacuum cleaners, describe them in detail. If you are opening a candy store, say what kind of candy you will offer (prepackaged or home-made chocolates or imported sweets). You need not list each individual variation of chocolate.

Describe peripheral items. Perhaps your stationery store also offers coffee and donuts for morning commuters. If you sell widgets, perhaps you sell a special installation kit, or a widget cleaning kit. Your car wash might sell after-market items, snacks, and drinks.

2. Services: What Service Do You Offer?

Describe your core services. For example, a dry cleaning business's core services might include standard cleaning, a leather and suede service, a sleeping bag and down comforter service, and special one-hour speed services.

Describe your peripheral services. A peripheral service "comes along" with other major items. For example, if your major product is a widget, peripheral services might include delivery, installation, routine servicing, warranty repairs, extended warranty repairs, and an annual inspection.

3. The Need: What Customer Needs Do These Products and Services Fill?

Describe what value your products or services give to your customers. If you expect people to pay good money for these offerings, the products and services must return some value. Types of needs can include the obvious direct use needs (they eat it, sit on it, wear it), and harder to define needs (emotional value, sex appeal, time saving, tension reduction). If the need is common, a simple statement of the existence of the need in your market will suffice.

If the need is new, if you are trying to artificially create a need, or if the need is not well known to the general population, you may want to dedicate a paragraph or more to an explanation.

4. Changes: What Changes Do You Anticipate to Your Offerings?

Adaptation in a changing marketplace is often vital for continued success. If you build off-road mountain bikes, but see a trend developing where commuters use these bikes around town, you might begin to change your product to adapt to this new need. You might offer generators and lights for night commuting, a new handlebar option for more comfortable road-riding, and easily interchangeable sets of on-road and off-road wheels.

If you run a catering service, you might find that your competitors are raking in the bucks by offering short-notice summer barbecues. You might counter this advantage by offering your own short-notice services, and by expanding the geographical range of your services. By anticipating these future adaptations into your business plan now, you can begin to plan for the additional advertising, equipment, vehicles, and employees you will need.

An immediate advantage of this "future thinking" is that you will show your potential lenders that you are intent on succeeding in the long run, and that your flexibility and planning in these real-market conditions will help ensure both your success and the viability of their loan to you.

"PRODUCTS/SERVICES" WORKSHEET

Products (core, peripheral):

Services (core, peripheral):

Needs:

Changes:

(Work space)

CREATE "MARKETS" AND "COMPETITION" SECTIONS

WHO YOU WILL SELL TO

The future success of your business (and the success of your loan application) will depend on how well you analyze two very important questions. Regardless of whether you produce Chocolate Covered Crunch Bombs cereal for kids, or run an exclusive men's tailoring shop, you must research and answer these questions if you want to be sure of success. They are deceptively simple:

> *To whom will I sell my product?*

> *Will they buy it?*

The first task of the markets section of your business plan is to identify to whom you will sell your product or service. This group of people is referred to as your "market segment." There are many ways to isolate this particular group from the rest of the general population and target your marketing efforts toward them effectively.

The second task is to determine if, why, and under what conditions they will buy your product. Again there exist specific techniques you can use to determine what will make these people buy your product.

If you target your product to the correct markets, it will probably sell. If you pick the wrong markets you will be throwing your hard-earned money away. Consequently, your lenders will look very closely at your market study.

CONTENTS OF "MARKETS"

What Group

What segment of the population will you sell to?

The idea here is to find as many criteria as possible which distinguish your buyers from the rest of the 4 billion people on earth. Young or old? Rich or poor? White collar or blue collar? Football watchers or backpackers? Male or female?

Why This Group

Why will they in particular buy your product?

You need to determine why this particular group is the best target for your marketing efforts (or whether some other group might be better). The more tightly you focus your efforts toward people who are very interested in your product, and the less you target people who are only mildly interested or indifferent, the more effective your advertising dollars will be and the more you will sell.

How You Will Motivate Them

*What will you do to influence them
to fork over their cash?*

Know your market. Certain things "wind their spring," while they will ignore most everything else. Sex sells more cars than safety. Ease of use, savings, image, and many other motivators can be effective under the right circumstances. What will work best to sell your product to your market?

Their Accessibility

Can you reach your markets with your product?

Here are two contrasting examples: If you cook and deliver Chinese food in Tucson, Arizona, the market of Chinese food lovers in New York City is logistically not accessible to you. However, if you catch and sell fresh Alaskan king crab in Alaska, people in New York will indeed pay large sums of money for your live crabs, and hence these people are accessible (via overnight airmail — no joke!).

What They Will Pay

What is the market willing to pay for your product?

Most often the price of a product is set by the market. By studying competitors' similar products, you can get an accurate feel for what the market will bear.

"MARKETS" EXAMPLES

[Example # 1]

QUICKEST COPY PHOTOCOPY SERVICE

Quickest Copy provides photocopying services to students at the University of Massa-

chusetts. Located between campus and the main off-campus living and shopping areas near downtown Amherst, it provides convenient service along the student's daily walk to school. Approximately 24,000 students between the ages of eighteen and twenty-four occupy the campus a quarter-mile from the shop. Classes routinely require students to photocopy work packets and other information.

In addition, Quickest Copy serves the downtown Amherst business community of about seventy small businesses, most of which are too small to be able to afford their own photocopiers, and the other 15,000 permanent residents of the area.

Current market prices for black-and-white photocopies run between 3 cents and 6 cents per page. Quickest Copy, because of its strategic location and lack of neighboring competition, will charge 5 cents per page.

[Example # 2]

LYCRA LAND CLOTHING

Lycra Land will market its running, bicycling, swimming and exercise apparel primarily to active and sports-conscious females and males between the ages of ten and forty. Boulder, Colorado is a sports mecca where over 600 cyclists and runners routinely exercise along the seven-mile Boulder Creek

Path during lunch each day, according to last year's city government study. Most are upper-middle class, health-conscious, and regard their sports clothing as status and social symbols.

The total population of the town is about 60,000. Recent polls by the Boulder Daily Camera indicate that over 60 percent of the population has moved to Boulder from other towns outside of Colorado. One of the primary reasons given by most people on why they chose Boulder was that it was a sports-oriented town with easy access to the nearby Rocky Mountains.

The mean income level of Boulderites is about $35,000 per year. Sports clothing is not only desirable to them, but easily affordable. Lycra Land will price its clothing about 5 percent higher than the stores in Crossroads mall to offset the high shop rental costs.

Lycra Land is to be located on the downtown Pearl Street Mall, in the heart of the walking and shopping district of town. Pedestrian traffic is heavy along the mall, which is used year-round by students and the working class for lunch and evening strolls as well as for shopping.

NOTE: Whenever citing specific information, like mean income levels or poll results, always remember to attribute the information in the body of your text and always include copies of the source material at the back of your presentation. Doing so makes you look thorough and professional.

HOW TO WRITE YOUR OWN "MARKETS" SECTION

1. Who are your markets geographically? (Local, state, USA, North America, Europe, etc.)

2. Who are your markets economically? (White collar, blue collar, ultra-rich — try to specify an income range.)

3. What is your market's age range? (Children, teens, college students, working people, retirees.)

4. Who are your markets socially? (Yuppies, dating singles, party hounds, domestics, football-watchers, travelers, sports players, drinkers.)

5. What do your markets do with their time? (Work, play team sports, raise kids, study in school, watch TV.)

6. What groups are you targeting? (Businesses, schools, leisure-time users, vacationers, diners, sex-crazed teenagers, sex-starved adults.)

7. What other characteristics make your markets stand out from the general population? (Health, diet, politics, propensity for gadgets, interest in science.)

8. Are your markets accessible? (You may not be able to deliver pizzas to a military base, for example.)

9. Through what mechanism will you interact with your markets? (Retail shops, personal delivery, door-to-door sales, mail order.)

10. What ways will you use to motivate this particular group of people to consume your product? Unless you motivate them, they won't part with their hard-earned dollars, even if they are interested in your product. There may be many effective motivators. (Suburbanites for example spend an inordinate amount of time caring for grass. A lawn service saves them time, sweat, bug bites, and does such a good job at it that they will be the envy of all their neighbors. Plus, it shows that they have money and don't have to mow their own grass.)

11. Will your markets accept your product or service? (Many college kids eat pizza, but fewer elderly people are interested.)

12. What is the size of the market? (Are there enough automobiles in your town to support the three existing car washes and your new car wash?)

13. What is the market's durability? (People bought Pet Rocks heavily for a short while, but the fad soon faded. On the other hand designer clothing, though it changes color and style faster than a chameleon, has a very durable market.)

14. Will the market grow or shrink? (As businesses become faster paced, the market for fax ma-

chines is growing dramatically. When the oil bust hit Denver, the housing market collapsed. What will your market do in the next five or ten or twenty years?)

15. What barriers must you overcome to open up your market? (For example, you might have to mount a publicity campaign to convince a skeptical public that your "platinum catalytic gas mileage enhancer carburetor insert" significantly improves mileage and that it's not just another example of automotive snake oil. Or you might need to find ways to change the ingredients used in your restaurant's recipes to cater to an increasingly large health-food conscious market segment.)

16. What product prices will your market bear? (Check competitors' stores in your area and in communities with similar market segments.)

"MARKETS" WORKSHEET

Distinguishing characteristics that describe your market segment.

Accessibility:

Interaction mechanisms:

Motivational approach:

Product acceptance by the market:

Market size, durability, and expansion/contraction:

Potential barriers to this market:

Product pricing:

(Work space)

ANALYZE YOUR COMPETITORS

For every business, competition is a fact of life. When you start your new business, you will have to deal with this fact, too. Your competitors may be staring at you from across the street or they may be located across the country at the other end of an 800 number. Even if you seem to have no competition right now (an enviable position!), your success will probably spur other entrepreneurs or larger businesses to move in to your territory.

In order to succeed, you must plan how you will take customers away from your competition and keep them for yourself. At trade fairs and flea markets you can actually watch aggressive sellers drag bewildered customers away by the arm from their competitors. In most businesses, however, the battle strategies are much more subtle. Advertising and publicity are the weapons of choice. The more skill with which you wield these tools, the more successful you will be and the more money you will make.

You must know your competition. And you must plan and act to defeat them. The "Competition" section of your business plan is for precisely this purpose. In it you will analyze your competitors and begin to develop battle strategies. You will finish the job in the "Marketing" section by laying out detailed plans for advertising, publicity, and sales. The planning you do in these two sections will act as a real-life, functioning, and evolving battle plan for your business.

CONTENTS OF "COMPETITION"

Your Competitors

Who are they?

Examine their size, location, product line, image, and all the other aspects of their business.

Their Products

What products and services do they offer?

Examine the differences and similarities in their products and services and your own. Compare cost, quality, durability, selection, and other criteria to see how they stack up against each other.

Their Strategies

What are their business goals?

Are they a mom-and-pop operation which may not see much growth; are they a big chain store which is slow to adapt; are they an aggressive and fast-moving outfit like yourself?

Their Markets and Marketing

What groups of people make up their markets?

Try to determine what groups they are selling to. Are those groups the same as yours, or do they only partially overlap? How much of the "market-share" do they have?

Their Advantages

What can they do better than you can do?

Compare size, financial backing (chains can have tremendous financial resilience), location, easy access to ample parking, nearby draws (other adjacent stores which attract customers), advertising, and so on. List their major strengths.

Your Advantages

What can you do better than they can do?

List your strengths. Maybe you are more adaptable, have a better location, or can more easily vary your product line to meet changing market conditions than they can. Perhaps you can just be friendlier and provide better customer service.

Their Weaknesses

What things are they failing to do well?

Try to spot holes in their market coverage, their advertising schemes, their location, and other facets of their business. This is an important step, since it lets you target your efforts to the weaknesses in their defenses.

Your Weaknesses

What things are you failing to do well?

Along the same line, by spotting your own weaknesses, you can begin to form plans to plug your holes and shore up your defenses. You should be constantly analyzing the weaknesses and strengths of your business and your competitors' even after you start your business. As you gain a larger share of the market, your competitors will almost certainly respond with a counter-move. Then you respond to their move. This game is the norm in the American marketplace.

Your Battle Plan

How will you attack your competition?

Now that you have a feel for the balances of strengths and weaknesses, you must determine how you will exploit your best advantages and your competitors' worst disadvantages. Perhaps you can distribute coupons through direct-mail coupon booklets or advertise on morning radio to commuters. As an example, when one old hotel in Leadville, Colorado began major refurbishment, its competitor countered the threat with extremely heavy cable television ads in the nearby Denver area. The effect was that everyone who watched cable knew the name of the advertising hotel, while few people recognized the name of the soon-to-be-opened, refurbished hotel.

Their Likely Response

How will they respond to your attack?

Chances are that if your competitors are small they will respond quickly, and if they are large their counter-move will be slower. But you can be sure that if you successfully pose a threat to their business, they will respond. Try to determine what they might do, and prepare your own next moves.

"COMPETITION" EXAMPLES

[Example # 1]

CONTINENTAL CUISINE CATERING

The main competition to Continental Cuisine comes from another local catering company called "An Elegant Dish" and the Italian catering department of Longmont's Rocky Mountain Hotel.

An Elegant Dish specializes in dinner parties to upper-middle class residents of Longmont and its surrounding residential areas. They offer high quality traditional American fare at reasonable prices, and have so far done a thriving business. The main weaknesses in their service are a lack of entertainment, sound systems, and other peripheral services. As a full-service caterer, Continental Cuisine will fill this need by offering a full spectrum of food, entertainment, and event coordination. Our advantage is that we handle the entire event for our customers, instead of simply the food portion of the event. This leaves customers free to host their guests and enjoy the event without worrying about coordinating the details.

The Rocky Mountain Hotel's main advantage over us is that they have a long-standing reputation for excellent food in their "Gianni's" Italian restaurant located in the hotel. To increase profits four years ago, they added an Italian catering service to their in-house restaurant. Their business works well as a complement to the restaurant, grossing an estimated $30,000 per year. Their main weakness, however, is their limited cuisine. Since Continental Catering offers a much wider selection of ethnic cuisines, it can capture a larger share of the catering market.

Continental Cuisine is starting a multi-media advertising campaign directed at Longmont residents and residents of the four smaller surrounding communities. The campaign will focus on our full-event services and our wide range of cuisines. This exploits both our strengths and our competitor's weaknesses.

In response to our campaign, The Rocky Mountain Hotel can do little in the way of changing its fare. An Elegant Cuisine, however, may decide to add other peripheral services to its current menu. Our tactics here include searching out and influencing as many of the local entertainers as we can reach immediately, and getting them on our bandwagon before An Elegant Cuisine can respond. We will also attempt to photograph our first few major local events for use in our advertising campaign, and will offer a discount to customers who agree to act as references for our new clientele. This forms a self-reinforcing network of contacts throughout the community.

[Example # 2]

LYCRA LAND CLOTHING

Lycra Land has two main groups of competitors in Boulder. The first group consists of some six bicycling stores and four camping goods stores. All of these stores offer Lycra body-wear and swimwear, and have steady clientele drawn by the various types of hardware they offer. Each store grosses between $50,000 and $150,000 per year.

The main weakness common to all these competitors is the fact that they have a limited stock of styles, colors, and sizes. Much of their space and capital are used for other products. Lycra Land will use this weakness by offering only body- and swimwear, and will have a large selection of styles, colors, and sizes. Human physiques and human tastes vary considerably in a town of 60,000, and our wide selection will draw customers who cannot find what they are looking for elsewhere. A second weakness of our competitors is that they are scattered around the fringes of the city.

Lycra Land will be located on the downtown Pearl Street Mall which has very heavy pedestrian traffic year-round. The drawback of this location is its high rental cost. Our financial studies based on the high traffic volume, however, indicate a short start-up period at this location in spite of its cost, achieving break-even in about two months.

The second group of competitors consists of the department and specialty stores in Crossroads Mall, many of whom offer the same large selection of body- and swimwear that we do. We will counter this threat by advertising on cable television on MTV and on CNN, the two channels most heavily watched by our market-segment. We will promote both our large selection (countering the advantages of the first group above) and our excellent location. The location close to campus and student's recreational activities (bars, shopping, restaurants) and to the majority of other small businesses in Boulder is without question the best in town. The ad's visual vehicle will use the sexiness of our young, upper-middle class customers in the setting of our Pearl Street Mall location to confer a sense of social exhilaration.

HOW TO WRITE YOUR OWN "COMPETITION" SECTION

1. Who are your competitors? (Name, address, description of location, size, financial state, and backing. Start by looking through the *Yellow Pages*, local newspapers, magazines, and coupon booklets. Then, if you might have competitors further afield, examine national ads, and

possibly international ads as well. If your competitors are doing a good advertising job, you will be able to find them easily.)

2. What are their products? (Types, quality, quantity, layout, selection or sizes and styles, cost, availability.)

3. What are their strategies? (High growth/unstable, measured growth/low risk, slow/ponderous/non-adaptable, mom-and-pop, no growth, quick-profits then crash-and-burn.)

4. Who are their markets? (Economic, age, sex, social group, working group, geographic location, growing or shrinking, durability, market-share.)

5. How do they reach those markets? (Walk-in, newspapers, magazines, television, radio, free publicity, sidewalk displays, telephone solicitation, direct mail.)

6. What are their advantages? (How they appeal to their markets, their size, financial backing, location, style, quality, cost, delivery, etc.)

7. What are your advantages? (How you appeal to your markets, your size, financial backing, location, style, quality, cost, delivery, etc.)

8. What are their weaknesses? (Marketing strategies they are missing, untapped market segments, lack of aggressiveness, slow to adapt, fixed product line, poor quality, low availability, high location cost, lack of public awareness.)

9. What are your weaknesses? (Marketing strategies they are missing, untapped market seg-

ments, lack of aggressiveness, slow to adapt, fixed product line, poor quality, low availability, high location cost, lack of public awareness.)

10. What is your battle plan? (How you intend to shore up and eliminate your weaknesses, and how you intend to exploit your competitors' weaknesses.)

11. What future moves can you predict from both sides? (Expansion, additional advertising, refining of product lines, legal attacks, location changes, sales events, etc.)

"COMPETITION" WORKSHEET

Competitors:

Products:

Strategies:

Markets:

Marketing:

Their advantages:

Your advantages:

Their weaknesses:

Your weaknesses:

Your battle plans:

Future moves:

(Work space)

Step Three

CREATE A "PRODUCTIONS" SECTION

HOW YOU WILL MAKE YOUR PRODUCT

The productions section of your business plan details how you will create the finished products which you are going to sell. Start-up costs for equipment, buildings, and inventory represent a significant investment in money and time. But just how much?

The productions section helps you analyze the tasks, equipment, employees and other facets of the production process for which you will have to shell out your precious start-up money. It also takes a look at your day-to-day operations and their costs. By examining these details now, you answer several questions important to both you and your lenders:

"How will I make my product?"
"What do I need to do the job?"
"What will be my start-up costs?"
"What will be my operating costs?"

In examining these questions you will develop a production plan, employee plans, financial plans, and a good idea of how you will schedule you company's start-up.

CONTENTS OF "PRODUCTIONS"

Raw Materials ==>	Production Tasks = = >	Finished product
materials	task flow	quality control
sources/selection	materials	flow packaging
cost	employees	storage
delivery	equipment	inventory
quality control	buildings	
inventory	red-tape	
costs		
other resources		
timing		

We will split the productions section into three separate steps:

- **Raw Materials** analyzes what you need, where you will get those items, and how much they will cost.
- **Production Tasks** looks at what you do to your raw materials in the way of processing, what equipment and employees you will need, how tasks flow together, and how materials move through theoperation.
- **Finished Product** examines what happens to the finished product before it is sold. It must be checked for quality, packaged, and stored in preparation for transport. We will examine marketing, sales, and shipping of the product in subsequent chapters.

EXAMPLE

CONTINENTAL CUISINE CATERING

Continental Cuisine will begin operations on October 1, 1992, serving residents and businesses of Longmont, Colorado. Advertising will have begun two weeks previously, and *Yellow Pages* ads will have been out for about one month. For an initial two-week shake-down period we plan to run at about 60 percent capacity, increasing to 100 percent capacity.

When each catering job is booked, we and the customer together prepare a menu and schedule for his or her event. Up to two weeks before the event he can cancel with a 40 percent fee. If he cancels during the last two weeks before the event he forfeits his deposit and full payment.

Continental Cuisine breaks down the customer's menu into raw materials. Non-perishables are ordered for delivery one week before the event, and perishables one to two days before the event for maximum freshness. Raw materials are inspected for quality, quantity, and proper selection upon arrival, then they are logged, then stored on stockroom and cold-storage shelves dedicated to that particular job. (This prevents materials from one job getting mixed up with those of other jobs.) Under full operations, Continental Cuisine will need 200 square feet of stockroom space (shelved). This will cost $2,200 in shelving and outfitting costs (one time), plus $200 per month in floor-space. We will also require 75 square feet of cold-storage, costing $4,000 to install, and $175 per month in floor-space and cooling costs.

The raw materials themselves will be ordered from local bulk foods distributors, including Pace warehouses and King Soopers. Staffing of the preparation, event and cleanup is scheduled about one week before the event.

Soups, desserts, and similar foods will be prepared ahead of time at Continental

Cuisine's kitchens. These kitchens will cover about 700 square feet and cost some $12,000 to set up, and $400 in floor-space and utilities per month to run. Entrees will be prepared at the customer's location prior to and during the event. This provides visual value to the guests as well as extremely fresh food. Continental Cuisine will start with two mobile kitchens costing $1,600 each. By re-investing profits heavily, we will increase the number over a period of one year to five kitchens. These kitchens include all food transport, preparation, and cleanup materials.

Special event hardware such as sound systems, large numbers of tables and chairs, risers, and bandstands will be rented for each event, limiting the company's equipment investment and passing the cost on to the customer. Centerpieces will be supplied and delivered by local floral wholesale distributors in the Denver area.

HOW TO WRITE YOUR OWN "PRODUCTIONS" SECTION

Raw Materials

Materials:

What raw materials do you need to make your product?

If you are selling clothing, your raw materials will be the clothing which you buy wholesale from various producers around the country or around the world. If you are selling a widget, your raw materials will be all the various parts which make up the widget, and all the peripheral parts needed, such as grease, solder, and tape. Indicate which of your raw materials, if any, are perishable.

Sources/Selection:

Where will you obtain your raw materials?

Here is where comparison shopping can save you a great deal of money. Find as many sources for your raw materials as possible. Compare quality, durability, cost, delivery time, payment schedules, payment method, and any other criteria which may apply. Remember that you don't necessarily have to get all your products from one source (though that simplifies bookkeeping). Carefully weigh each source's merits. Then make a list by product, indicating your first and second choice sources. The second choice is important in case your main supplier has sudden problems. Write down how you will order each item (phone, mail, fax) and the appropriate addresses and telephone numbers for ordering. Now try to make a rough estimate of the labor costs (in hours per month and in dollars per month) spent ordering your raw materials.

Cost:

How much will your raw materials cost?

For each raw item, list its name, unit size, weight, bulk or other characteristics (whichever is appropriate), and the unit cost. If you are making widgets, now list how many widgets you can make with one unit measure of the item. (This is not necessary with simple retail sales items).

Delivery:

How will your raw materials be delivered?

For each raw item, list the delivery method, the delay between ordering and delivery, the delivery cost, and the deliverer.

Quality Control:

When an item is delivered, how will you check it?

Explain what your delivery-acceptance procedure entails. It should probably contain the following steps: check the item's type, quantity, color, size, freshness, visible damage, and check these against what you actually ordered. You may have ordered three cases of red men's BVDs, but received three cases of red women's panties instead. Once an item passes inspection, log it in your delivery book, along with the date, time, and who accepted the delivery. This important step helps catch and prevent missing shipments and employee pilferage. Determine what your labor costs will be for the delivery-acceptance and quality control time spent each month.

Inventory:

How do you keep track of your raw materials?

Materials arrive, they are processed, they are stolen, they are broken or damaged, and they must be reordered at the appropriate time. How will you keep track of inventory? Small operations use a simple notebook or file cards. Large operations with hundreds or thousands of parts often need a computerized inventory program. Determine how you will keep inventory and what your costs will be in equipment and monthly labor. Now determine what amount of space you will need for your raw material inventory. If you have a particular building in mind for your business, determine how much this square-footage will cost you per month.

Production Tasks

Tasks:

How will you turn raw materials into finished products?

List each of the steps you must take to turn your raw materials into your finished, saleable product. These might include physical steps (cooking, bolting, soldering, molding), or time-steps (waiting for food to marinate, waiting for a chemical reaction to occur or a cast part to cool). Pure-retailers must hang or shelve their products, create displays, etc. (Retailers of pre-made goods will find these production steps trivial.)

For manufacturers, this can be a very complicated step to figure out. One easy way is to diagram it, starting with your raw materials on the left, and ending with your finished product on the right. See the next page for a simple example.

Example of a Simple "Production Flow Diagram" To Make A Pepperoni Pizza

```
FLOUR --------\
WATER ----------\
BAKING SODA -------\
BAKING POWDER -------|--MAKE PIZZA DOUGH--\
TOMATO SAUCE ------------------------|--ADD SAUCE--\
PEPPERONI --------------------------------\
CHEESE -------------------------------------|--ADD TOPPINGS
                                              --BAKE--SLICE
```

Task Flow:

In what order must these tasks be done?

When creating this type of diagram, sort the tasks you listed in the previous step into their correct order of occurrence (you can't add the sauce until you have made the dough). Now, annotate the diagram with the quantity of each raw item needed for one finished item. Finally indicate the time and employees needed for each step.

Materials Flow:

How do materials move from the stockroom through production?

This is essentially traffic planning. If you want to make wooden tables at home, will you have to carry lumber from your storage area in the garage through the kitchen to the basement wood shop? What will your family say? Can you get the finished table back up the basement stairs and through the door? While this example is simple, traffic planning of materials and people can have very major effects in many cases. Restaurants, for example, have solved nasty personnel problems by rearranging the kitchen so that food and people flow logically and without hindering each other.

Employees:

What employees are needed in the production process?

For each step of the production process, list who does it, how much time they will spend (per finished item), what their skills must be, and what dangers are involved. Find out from your local job-search organizations and employment agencies if people with these skills are available in your area and how much they cost per hour.

Equipment:

What equipment is needed for the production process?

This one may take you some time, because it is a very important step. Mentally walk through the production process and visualize each and every piece of equipment you will need (from major expenses down to carrot-peelers and brooms — the costs all add up). List them all. Now comparison shop to find the best deals for each item. Add to your list each item's price and where you found the best deal.

Buildings/Space:

What floor-space will you need and where?

The amount of space you require may grow as your business grows. Take into account your current needs for production space, raw materials storage space, finished product storage space, management space, and employee space. How about parking lots, driveways, and loading areas? Location is very important for retail sales, and less important for manufacturing. How will your possible location affect your customers? When you calculate building costs include one-time costs (down-payment, security deposit, remodeling) and monthly payments (mortgage, rent, electricity, gas, water/sewer, maintenance, insurance, etc.).

Red Tape:

What permits, licenses, and other documents do you need?

Restaurants need certification/inspection and alcohol licenses. Car washes may need waste water treatment and recycling systems on-site. Check out the local and state building codes, business licenses, fees, and restrictions well in advance of deciding on a final location.

Other Resources:

What other materials, resources, and skills will you need?

Some businesses need seasonal labor, subcontractors, consultants, and other special resources.

Timing:

What are your production timing considerations?

This is very dependent on the type of business you operate. If you are competing for half-hour pizza delivery, your production timing is critical. If you are selling retail, your special ordering may be time-critical. Retail stores often plan many months ahead for seasonal sales, such as Thanksgiving and Christmas. What are your particular timing needs?

Finished Product

Quality Control:

What determines if your finished product is fit to sell?

American consumers are highly quality conscious, and virtually all production companies have some form of product inspection. Develop pass/fail criteria for your product. If a damaged or poor product reaches a customer, what are his rights, warranties, and guarantees? What are your repair policies? What are your replacement policies? What are their costs?

Packaging:

How will you wrap your finished product?

Few products go out the door "naked." Packaging not only protects the product, it provides consumer information, and advertises for you. How will you package the final product? What will that packaging say? How will it effectively protect the product during storage and transport? What are your per-unit packaging costs? Is your packaging environmentally sound?

Storage:

What storage space will your finished products need?

Products often sit around in inventory after they have been produced and before they are delivered. How much space will they require? Will you need shelves, refrigerators, fork lifts or loading docks?

Inventory:

How will you keep track of finished products?

We will cover sales and transport later. For now, you need to think about how you will store, catalog, and inventory your finished products. Inventory is important for both ordering purposes and for detecting theft.

"PRODUCTIONS" WORKSHEET

Materials:

Sources/selection:

Cost:

Delivery:

Quality control:

Inventory:

Tasks:

Task flow:

Materials flow:

Employees:

Equipment:

Buildings/space:

Red tape:

Other resources:

Timing:

Quality control:

Packaging:

Storage:

Inventory:

(Work space)

Step Four

CREATE A "MARKETING" SECTION

OPEN YOUR CUSTOMERS' WALLETS

The marketing section of your business plan describes what specific methods you will use to reach your customers, inform them of your products, and motivate them to buy from you.

In the previous "Markets" section, you identified your market segment (to whom you will sell), and what your competition will be like. Then in the "Products" section you analyzed your products, their strengths and their faults. Now you will take what you learned about your markets and your products and create specific advertising and publicity schemes to connect your product with your customers.

CONTENTS OF "MARKETING"

Methods

Many methods are available to reach your market segment. These could include direct mail, television, radio, newspaper ads, magazine ads, and other methods. Below, we will examine each of the popular marketing methods and their characteristics.

Cost

The cost of each method varies with its type, who you are trying to reach, and when, and with how much force.

Cost Effectiveness

For each dollar you spend to reach, inform, and influence your customers, how effective is your return? How many customers actually buy your product? The customer-draw per advertising dollar can vary dramatically, and it is important to know what it is so you can get the maximum bang for your buck.

Feedback

In order to make the most of your limited advertising dollars, you should monitor how effective they are. Feedback is how to put your cost-effectiveness research into practice.

GET FREE PUBLICITY

One good source of free publicity is the review. You can invite members of the local press to events, offering free meals or other gifts, and in return get a review of your service. This works well for restaurants. Needless to say, invite them to your best events, where your services display excellence in every aspect. The press is just as likely to give a scathing review of a bad service as it is likely to give a good review of a good service; but bad reviews are remembered longer than good ones.

THE YELLOW PAGES

The *Yellow Pages* will most likely be your single most important place to advertise, since this is where most consumers and other potential customers automatically turn first for information. Take some time to analyze what size ads you can afford. There are two places a business can be listed: in the *Yellow Pages* ad section and in the White Pages. You should do both, since a person may remember the name of your business and find it most easily in the *White Pages* first. Conversely, if someone doesn't know of your business, he will see the listing in the *Yellow Pages*.

In-line listings, using the normal small print, are generally referred to as "courtesy listings" and are free for both phone book sections. Display ads are the credit-card sized or larger boxes which contain text and graphics. While these may be expensive, they are probably your single best advertising investment.

You may be able to get free courtesy listings in other nearby phone books just by asking. For example, if you advertise in the Boulder, Colorado directory, you are also entitled to free courtesy listings in the much larger Denver phone directory. This is a powerful way to broaden your geographical coverage at no extra charge.

When planning *Yellow Pages* ads, remember that while the directory charges you a monthly fee, you may have to pay for twelve months of ad space, because the next directory will not be issued for a year. The publishers of the directory will help you create the ad — this service is usually included in your base price for the ad space.

DISPLAY ADS

Display ads in magazines and newspapers are large, often colorful quarter-, half- or full-page ads. They command attention. You use display ads:

1. When you need to use a photo or illustration to show what your service is, or to give a mood or feel to your service.

2. When you want to attract attention and receive more orders.

3. When your service appeals to a large percentage of the readership.

4. When you need the space to tell the complete story about your service, such as a bulleted list of functions (weddings, lunches, barbecues, etc.).

What is the secret to successful display advertising? It's really no secret at all. All it takes are three things.

1. You've got to offer a service or product that people want, or at least think they want.

2. You've got to know when and where to advertise your catering service — which magazine or newspaper to use and which month to run your ad.

3. Your ad must motivate people to take action.

Since people are barraged with advertisements of all types, try to make your ad stand out. Use typestyles, pictures, formats, and layouts that are different from your competitors' ads. You must make your readers stop turning the pages and look at your ad. Like the farmer said when he hit his mule over the head with a two-by-four, "You have to get its attention first."

Next try to evoke a mood with your ad. People are emotionally motivated more easily than logically motivated (though you will need to use both). Clothing and car dealers alike use sex appeal to sell their products. Adult cereal ads use pastoral shots of fields of grain to evoke a mood. What emotions are appropriate to both your product and your customers?

Analyze who your customers are and cater to their specific needs. What are those needs? Cost savings, social gratification, efficiency, speed, or something else? You must solve their problem, even if it is a problem they don't yet know they have. Think about all the deodorant ads you see. Are Americans really that smelly? Or have the deodorant producers simply encouraged us to think so?

Finally, motivate them to buy your product. Ask them in some forceful way to open their wallet. Better yet, tell them to fork over the cash. If they don't, what horrible things are going to happen to them? ("If you don't buy Zittoff skin cream, you'll never, ever get a date again in your life!" "If you don't use Continental Cuisine Catering, your party will be a flop, you'll lose your friends to food poisoning, and you'll have to move out of state to avoid jail!") These aren't literally the things you'll say, of course, but the implication will be there.

If this sounds cynical, take a hard look at magazine ads. The more effective the ad, the better it is using these techniques.

To choose periodicals in which to advertise your product, think about what magazines and newspapers are most read by your market segment. Target those people as closely as possible. You ad money will be wasted if you advertise in magazines which are not read by your market segment. Before placing a classified advertisement, you need to determine what publications are good bets:

1. Make a list of all your possible types of customers.

2. Go to the newsstand and make a list of all periodicals that cover your geographic area.

3. Trim your list of publications to only those which already run ads for products or services similar to yours.

The cost of display ads depends on several factors: the number of colors, the size of the ad, the circulation of the magazine, and the type of its readership. Contact the magazine's or newspaper's advertising department for specific rates.

CLASSIFIED ADS

Classified ads can be placed in most newspapers and magazines. Their cost varies with the circulation of the periodical and the amount of space each ad occupies.

You use classified ads:

1. When you want to receive inquiries from potential customers, you then follow up those inquiries with literature to close the sale.

2. To sell directly from the ad if your product costs from $1 to $5 (such as a lunch service or coffee service) — no more (as a rule).

Classified advertising is generally regarded as the least expensive way to advertise to the public. Not all publications carry a classified section, but there are enough of them available to sustain a major ad campaign. Aside from being low in cost, a classified ad is easiest to write and get into print, and is an inexpensive way to get experience in advertising.

Many newspapers now carry a special "business and service" section within their classified ads, in which local businesses such as painters, typing services, and gardening services advertise. These business sections stand out to the readers visually, and provide quick access to a variety of services. They are preferable to the standard classified section for several reasons:

1. Readers know exactly where to look for your service — your ad doesn't "get lost in the shuffle" of thousands of other ads.

2. Business classifieds are sold by the month.

3. Rates are often lower than for a standard classified ad, since the newspaper is selling you a month's space instead of a few days, as with most classified ads.

4. Many business classified sections allow small display ads, about one inch square, which make your service stand out visually.

The price of a classified advertisement is determined by the number of words or lines it contains. Some newspapers with small circulation charge by the line. The larger publications which charge on a per-word basis charge anywhere from $1 to $7 — or more — per word. The larger the circulation, the higher the per-word price. In a local paper with a circulation of about 30,000 readers, for example, the word-rate would be in the neighborhood of 25¢ to 55¢ per word. This low rate is due to the relative "overhead" costs of keeping that publication economically feasible. In a magazine with a circulation of about 3 million, such as a magazine specializing in a large city, like *The New Yorker*, word rates may range from $3 to $8 per word.

Although a publication distributes a certain number of a single issue, this does not mean that only a corresponding number of people will read it. If, for example, a monthly magazine claims three million copies sold per issue, statistics prove that an average of seven to nine million people will actually have read that issue. The magazine may be read by several members of a household, and perhaps by hundreds in a dentist's waiting room.

There are many publications in which you could advertise: several local newspapers, perhaps a local-area magazine, and even "free papers" which are distributed to the public free of charge at supermarkets and other shops.

Most periodicals demand cash, certified check, or credit card payment. Once you have established your good paying reputation and regularly insert your ad, some publishers will consider extending credit. They are certainly not obligated to do so, however.

Because most publications charge by the word for classified advertising, you will have to learn to write concisely, making every word work hard for the money. Your name and address will probably be five words, so the body of your ad will probably consist of another ten to fifteen words. When you write your ad, look carefully at each word. If it doesn't add significantly to the value of the ad, fix it.

Because most services require a telephone contact first to arrange the time, location, and content, include your phone number. You almost never ask for money in a clas-

sified ad. Your primary goal is to get the potential customer to call or write to you for information about your
services. Therefore, a key word in the ad is "free." Every-
body wants to receive something for nothing. Your offer
of free information in a classified will attract many responses because the reader figures he or she has nothing
to lose.

Classified advertising works, but takes a little time,
some testing, and some determination. The proof that it
pays off is the great number of classifieds that appear every
day in newspapers, and every week and month in magazines.

For a more complete analysis and instruction of classi-
fied ad writing, write for *How to Write A Classified Ad That
Pulls*, available for $3.25 from: Davis Publications, 380
Lexington Avenue, New York, New York, 10168-0035; Att:
Irene Bozoki.

DIRECT MAIL

Unquestionably, direct mail is the quickest way to get
your sales message into the hands of prospects or to test a
new idea. In direct mail, you send out information about
your product or products in the form of a sales letter, a
brochure, a flyer, or a catalog — or any combination of the
five. You send these mailings to the names of the people
on your mailing list. Where do you get the mailing list?
Either you compile the list yourself or you buy or rent a
mailing list. Obviously, if you are just starting out, you do
not yet have a list, so you must buy or rent a list, or do some
homework to compile one.

Be forewarned, however, that direct mail may not be a good idea for the beginner. For one thing, unless you are just sending out inexpensive flyers (the value of which may be questionable), it can be quite expensive. First you must buy or rent a mailing list from a qualified broker, then create an attractive, effective mailing piece, and then pay for all of those envelopes and postage. And remember that you can expect only a 2 to 3 percent response rate from such a mailing.

It is probably best to wait until you have compiled your own list of customers, then periodically send them material on your service.

Where to Get Mailing Lists

Mailing lists are available from list brokers or from other companies which sell by mail. A good broker will have access to mailing lists for every possible category of buyer. You can find mailing list brokers by looking in your nearest big city *Yellow Pages* under "Advertising — Direct Mail" or "Mailing Lists." You can also go to your library's reference section and locate a directory called *Direct Mail List Rates and Data*; it offers many sources of mailing lists and much helpful information.

When you rent a list, you are authorized to use that list only once. When you buy a list, you can use it as many times as you want; the catch is that it will become outdated.

Instead of using a broker, you can also rent a mailing list from another company that has sold successfully by mail.

To compile your own list, be inventive: who might need your services in the near future? If you cater weddings, for example, scan the local newspapers' wedding announcements sections and direct mail immediately to those couples. If you cater business lunches and meetings, direct mail to the "Events and Meetings Planner" of all the local companies over, say, 100 people. Also direct mail (especially in the spring) to every organization which holds company picnics, including town government, police, and other public organizations.

After a while, from your original sales and from those you make through other lists, you will have compiled the most valuable list there is: people who have hired your catering company in the past. This is the list you should use over and over again to get new jobs.

BULLETIN BOARDS AND HANDOUTS

Bulletin boards are of value for advertising certain types of products. Bulletin boards can be found in many public places, in office buildings, and in universities.

The advantage of bulletin boards is that you can post inexpensive flyers and even coupons without charge. The disadvantages are that your flyers may be covered by other people's flyers, that the boards can be cleaned off at random, and that they do not specifically target your market segment.

If you use bulletin boards, make sure that you do not violate any rules. For example, many boards within office buildings have specific purposes, such as for Equal Opportunity Employment, or for corporate notices.

Handouts are cheap and easily produced. They can be given to people attending specific events, such as trade fairs, conventions, movies, and rallies. However, they are often thrown away quickly. A 2 to 3 percent return for flyers is considered good.

FAX MACHINES

It's truly the yuppie generation. Office workers regularly use fax machines to communicate for business or personal use, ordering lunch, and ordering products. You might be able to tap into the fax network.

To do this, you need a fax machine and fax phone number, and some sort of faxable advertisement. Since a fax machine ties up one phone line, you should not use your normal business "voice" telephone line, but should instead get a separate line. Fax machines cost between four hundred and two thousand dollars, so you may want to wait a year or two before investing in one.

Fax machines are primarily useful for quickly sending your customers information which they have requested. If they are interested in your product, your ability to deliver quick price or product information into their hands can give you a great edge over your competitors.

You may have the urge to fire off unsolicited fax ads to potential customers. While this may get you some business, it will also generate a lot of hostility. Businesses and individual fax owners are besieged by fax ads and other junk mail which uses up their paper and toner, and wastes their time and money. Some communities and states are instituting legislation which would make it illegal to send unsolicited "junk fax mail."

RADIO ADS

Radio advertising has been quite successful in many industries. Its advantages include:

- Low cost.

- It reaches large numbers of potential customers.

- It can transmit an appropriate mood and feel of your product services.

- Ads can be changed quickly and cheaply to hit seasonal markets, or as your needs change.

- It has little lag time, unlike printed material which takes days or months to hit the newsstands.

Unfortunately, there are so many other ads competing for the attention of the consumer, that your ad may get lost if it fails to grab the listener's ear. Radio listeners cannot see your product, and their retention of audio messages is very limited compared with visual messages. However, there are a few ways you can make your ad stand out in the hodge-podge of radio commercials:

- Keep your message simple and straightforward, repeating the name of your company several times, and repeating one strong selling point over and over.

- Use a simple, easily remembered "jingle." These tunes, heard many times, will lodge in the dark recesses of listeners' brains for years, long after your name and message have been overrun with other commercials. Then, one "refresher" commercial later will make the listener recollect your previous ads.

- Send your message in terms your potential customers will understand and which set the tone of your product.

- Make your listener take immediate action to call you.

To target your markets, talk with the advertising director of the radio station and determine the time of day and day of the week the radio ads are to be broadcast. Are you trying for the business community? Rush hour, when they are all sitting in their cars, is a good time. Housewives? Try mornings, when housewives are doing chores with the radio on.

Since these "prime times" appeal to the needs of many advertisers, competition for these time slots has driven their price up. Evening ads and late night ads compete with television and sleep-time, and so are less desirable, but cheaper.

Before producing your radio commercial, listen to many other commercials with a critical ear. Which ones catch your attention, and which ones produce some sort of positive response in you? What characteristics enhance them? What characteristics detract from their selling power? Put together a list of characteristics which would suit your service, such as length of the commercial, length and use of the jingle, length and use of verbal text, type of voice used, tone of voice used, and time of day you heard the commercial. Since your advertisement depends heavily on the nature of your particular operation, you will have to mold these general guidelines into a specific radio "spot" for your own business. If you need more help, contact the radio station or a local ad agency which handles radio ads.

TELEVISION ADS

Television is a forceful advertising medium. Once, TV ads were reserved for big companies with large advertising budgets, who could claim the limited air time on the few channels which "free air broadcast." Cable has changed all this, because it has expanded the number of channels from four or five, to thirty or more. More channels mean more "ad slots" are available, which drives the price of ad-time down. It is routine to see local restaurants, vacuum cleaner stores, and other small businesses advertising continually. The advantages of television advertising over other forms of ads are:

- Both visual, audio, and text can be used.
- It uses motion to create excitement.
- Potential customers get an immediate feel for your business by watching examples of your product or service in action.
- Ads can be timed for upcoming seasons or events.

TV advertising is, however, expensive, especially during the prime-time hours when your markets are most likely to be watching.

Though small businesses can afford it, it may soak up pots full of your hard-won money quickly. The cost is set by the local cable company, and depends on what the market will bear, how large a viewership they have, the operating costs of the station, and how much competition exists for ad slots. However, if you have money available, TV advertising is a quick way to dramatically increase the number of customers who seek you out.

Be smart about doing a TV commercial: shell out the bucks and let the professionals handle it. When shopping for an ad agency, ask to see several other commercials they have produced. Do the commercials look second-rate compared with nationally produced commercials, or do they have that slick, snappy punch which will compete effectively? Comparison shop for ad agencies, considering both cost and quality.

STREET ADS

Street ads are effective because they carry a simple message, and are seen by the same people every day, over and over again. They include billboards, signs, "sandwich" boards, posters, and even murals. The cost of producing these ads is generally low, consisting of making the single copy of the ad, and hanging it somewhere appropriate. You might have to pay rent for the ad, but these costs are minimal compared with the more volatile advertising media like radio, television, and print.

Drawbacks to street ads include legislation to limit billboards and to control what you can put on street ads; and the fact that your ad is not tightly targeted toward your desired market, but seen by hundreds or thousands of people who couldn't care less.

To produce a street ad, first determine where you will place it, and how much space-rental will cost (if anything). Ads hung outside your shop are generally free, since you own or rent that space already. Billboards are not free — their price varies with location and competition for the billboard space. Take into account location, since this determines how many people will see the ad, and hence its effectiveness. Scope out each location — drive and walk by to see if your ad might be noticed. Ads near stop signs are more effective than ads placed on crowded 55 mph freeways, for example, since viewers have more "free time" to view the ad.

Design your ad. Keep text simple, since people passing by will probably read no more than three to five words. Include your company name, but not your telephone number, since the number will be forgotten immediately. Use a picture or a logo to lodge a visual image of your service in their minds. As examples of the effectiveness of logos, what companies use the "golden arches" and the "red star on a white background"? McDonald's and Texaco, of course!

Keep it short, bold, and simple. Use large, bold lettering which can be seen quickly from a distance. And don't let your ads weather and deteriorate, since this reflects poorly on your company's image.

TWEAK YOUR MARKETING WITH FEEDBACK

One important aspect of your marketing efforts, which you should include in your business plan, is the process by which you fine-tune your ads. "Feedback" is basically asking in some way, where your customers heard about your product or service.

Phone Responses—Ask Which Ad

When you receive phone responses to your ad, ask the potential customer where he or she heard about your business, and write down which publication or media it came from. In this way, you can keep a good record of which ads work best for you. The next time you sit down to buy more advertising space or air-time, you have statistics which tell you where your dollars have been most effective.

Written Responses — Key Your Ad

When placing an ad in more than one publication, it is important to "key" your ads. The "key" is a code used by mail order advertisers (in display advertising as well) to know from which ad the inquirer responded. The key is usually appended to the address like this:

> **John Smith Catering**
> **44 Adams Street**
> **Suite 110**
> **Merryland, CA 90909**

In the above example, "Suite 110" is the key used. Other keys common to classified ads are "Drawer ##" and "Dept. ##". Drawer is acceptable, but department sounds too office-like for a catering business. You can also use letters of the alphabet for methodical keying, like this:

> **John Smith Catering**
> **44-A Adams Street**
> **Merryland, CA 90909**

The "A" after the civil number is the key in this case. Your second ad would have a "B" instead of the "A," the third a "C," and so on.

An excellent keying method which cuts down record keeping work is the date and name of the magazine included in the ad like this:

John Smith Catering
44 Adams Street, #BG-7/10
Merryland, CA 90909

The BG in the drawer number in this case might represent *Boston Globe*, the periodical in which the ad appeared. The "7/10" refers to the issue date of the periodical, namely July 10th. Keying like this helps you keep accurate records of which ad works in which periodical, and in which issue.

Some people worry that they won't receive their mail if they include a foreign element on their address, such as a suite or other keying number. In reality, there is nothing to worry about because the post office will direct mail with a civil number and street name (or a P.O. Box number) disregarding the suite or drawer number.

EXAMPLES

[Example # 1]

CONTINENTAL CUISINE CATERING

Continental Cuisine will advertise in the White Pages and *Yellow Pages* of the Longmont, Denver, Boulder and surrounding communities. *Yellow Page* ads will be two inch by four inch display ads listed under

"Caterers." These ads will cost us approximately $400 per month.

In addition, we will advertise on local cable television during prime-time evening hours, approximately one month before the major holidays of Thanksgiving, Passover, and Christmas. We will also in January through April advertise our wedding banquet services in preparation for the popular spring wedding season. One hundred ad spots per month in the local area will cost us $750. Each ad will cost about $1,500 to produce. Since an "average" wedding banquet brings in $1,100, payback will be quick.

Once a customer has inquired about our services, we will immediately mail him a large-format brochure of our offerings. Employees will follow up on the brochure four days after mailing with personal telephone contacts. Repeat customers will be encouraged to again use our services by direct mail at four month intervals.

[Example # 2]

LYCRA LAND CLOTHING

Lycra Land's main advertising will be its store display window. Since over two thousand pedestrians pass the shop window each day, we will use a variety of sporting displays changed at one month intervals. We will rent sail-boards, kayaks, skis, bicycles, and other sporting equipment from the local stores at reduced rates, in return for placing their company sign with the equipment on display. Mannequins will be dressed in our clothing and poised in dynamic positions on the equipment.

In addition, Lycra Land will hold a weekend sale every two months. These sales will be advertised in the Boulder *Daily Camera*, and the Colorado *Daily* which is heavily read by the university students.

We will also explore placing a small "personals" ad in the local newspapers reading "Body Heat: increase your sexiness. Visit Lycra Land."

HOW TO WRITE YOUR OWN "MARKETING" SECTION

1. Which media are potentially suitable for your product or service? To be effective, these media must reach your market segment, must be able to carry information about your offering, and must be able to motivate your customers.

2. What size, length and sophistication of ad is it possible to place in each medium? Concentrate on the technical details here.

3. What are the costs of each of these ads and options? Make a table of costs for each particular media, and each size, length, and other criteria.

4. Which medium targets your market segment most closely? Some media are very broad, while some can focus in on particular groups of people.

5. Which medium reaches the most potential customers for the least cost? In other words, compare cost and effectiveness and determine which medium gives you the most bang for your buck.

6. What number, size, length, and cost ads will you place? Here you will have to juggle numbers. You may want to try several media on a small scale initially, then use feedback mechanisms to determine which has been most effective one or two months later.

7. What feedback mechanisms will you put in place to monitor the effectiveness of your ads? Your use of these mechanisms will influence lenders very positively, showing them that you adapt quickly to both positive and negative ad campaign results.

"MARKETING" WORKSHEET

1. Media suitable for your product or service:

2. Ad characteristics possible in each medium:

3. Ads/options costs:

4. Media which target your market segment best:

5. Most cost-effective media:

6. Ads—type, number, size, length, other characteristics:

7. Feedback mechanisms:

(Work space)

CREATE A "RISKS" SECTION

MAJOR HURDLES YOU MUST OVERCOME

Risks are essentially any thing or event which could keep you from achieving your business goals. Risks might be financial in nature, or be caused by a competitor, or even simply be the question of whether a new and unknown product will be accepted by consumers.

Obviously you can't predict all the risks to your business. When war broke out in the Middle East and the price of oil doubled, your plastics business may have become prohibitively costly through no fault of your own. However, many risks can be predicted before you ever lay down your cash to start your business. By identifying these risks now, you can plan how to limit your exposure, how to avoid certain risks, and how to overcome others when they arrive.

Engineers who design machinery and electronics regularly approach the creation of a new product with two important steps.

First, they analyze what problems and risks are inherent in their design. Second, they try to engineer out these problems during the design phase, before the product is even constructed. You should do the same thing with your new business plans. Examine your risks. Engineer out the ones you can, and make contingency plans for the others.

CONTENTS OF "RISKS"

You:

Are you really fit for this business? Your personality, your skills, your ability to solve problems, your devotion to your idea, and your proficiency in working with other people will all play an important part in your success. And you might get sick, with no one else to take the helm.

Employees:

Employees may lack work skills, people skills, dedication, or other abilities necessary to their job. They also rarely share your devotion to your business, and are more often "in it for the money."

Finances:

Do you have enough money to start your business, to keep it going, and to weather dry periods? Are your savings in a stable place? Could lawsuits bankrupt you?

Markets:

Can market fluctuations do you in? Is your market cyclic or seasonal? Is it shrinking? Does it really exist?

Competition:

Do your competitors have advantages which you cannot overcome?

Newness:

Are you offering a new product or service for which no market currently exists? Do you have to build up a need in the minds of your consumers?

Marketing:

Are you banking everything on an ad campaign which may or may not work?

EXAMPLES

[Example # 1]

CONTINENTAL CUISINE CATERING

One of the risks facing Continental Cuisine is based on the current economic situation of the country. Put simply, when the economy fluctuates downward, as it did with the Middle East crisis, people cut down on their purchases of non-essential services such as catering. Though the sources of this risk are out of our control, we will compensate with advertising to boost our sales of wedding banquets and buffets, which are affected far less by economic problems. People are almost always willing to spend a considerable amount of money for this once-in-a-lifetime experience.

A second risk is that of liability. Other catering companies have experienced on-site fires, water damage, and equipment injury. We will reduce the likelihood of these events with an employee training program which will include equipment-use and safety, and how to deal with guests at events (including belligerent and inebriated people). Continental Cuisine will also carry full damage and personal liability insurance to cover both our employees, our equipment, any guests or clients injured, and any client's property damaged.

[Example # 2]

THE SURF CAR WASH

The prime risk for The Surf is the weather. During periods of bad weather, few people wash their cars. Immediately after bad weather, when the roads dry, we have a large influx of customers. Within a week, this peak diminishes down to a standard low level of use. By locating in Colorado, the Surf takes advantage of the extremely variable weather patterns. Periods of bad weather generally last only one to three days, and are almost always followed by warm sunshine and quickly drying roads.

Competition provides a second risk. Three other car washes operate in town, at widely spaced locations. The Surf will encourage repeat business by giving every customer a 10 percent discount coupon, good for two months. Additional local cable television advertising will also give us a higher profile than that of our competitors.

The most serious risk is that we have a tight budget. If we fail to draw customers during

the first several months, we may default on
our loan payments. To counter this, we have
planned to book labor on a daily basis, using
the weather reports to predict how much
business we will have coming in. Since our
area has a good supply of unskilled labor-
ers, our pre-wash and drying crews can
range from three people on bad days, to
over forty people on post-storm days. We
will also run local cable television ads during morning pre-commute news hours, and
during evening news hours on CNN, since
the majority of our market segment is composed of working people who drive. We will
arrange to run these ads only on and after
bad-weather days, targeting our customers
when their awareness of their dirty cars is
highest.

HOW TO WRITE YOUR OWN "RISKS" SECTION

For your own risk analysis, think about the most likely
and the most damaging risks. Concentrate on these, rather
than on obscure and unlikely events. You need not write
down answers to all the questions here, just the ones which
are real risks for you. But think about them all.

1. **You:** Are you suited to your business? Do you
   have the necessary skills, and if not, how will
   you get them? How does your personality fit
   the job? If you are rubbed raw by certain tasks,
   you may be able to delegate them to employees.

Are you devoted to your idea? If not, you probably should not be starting the business. Do you have persistence, tenacity, and are you a problem solver? Such characteristics can certainly be developed, but starting a new business may be a rough way to attain them.

2. **Your family:** Are they supportive? Can they put up with the long hours, the financial insecurity, and other hardships which come with a new business? Family pressures can spell the doom of the family, the business, or both. However, by examining the potential problems and discussing them with all family members, including children, everyone will know what to expect, and can pull together. What steps will you take to minimize your family-oriented risks?

3. **Employees and partners:** How do they fit? You can limit these risks by carefully examining their skills and personalities before you ask them to join your organization. What questions will you ask and what research will you do on each potential employee or partner to minimize mismatch risks?

4. **Financial risks:** Can you get enough money to start your business and carry it and you through the first few months? Do you have secure savings to fall back on for emergencies? Are your loan payments dangerously high? Are you starting slow, or banking everything on the first few sales? Have you minimized your initial

expenses as much as possible, but not too much? How can you minimize these financial risks?

5. **Market risks:** Do your markets fluctuate seasonally, or with consumer whims, or with other events? Are your markets big enough to absorb you and your competitors? Are your markets growing or shrinking? Can your markets afford to buy your product in large quantity while giving you a profit? What events could cause your markets to dry up? How can you modify your market segment to avoid these problems?

6. **Competition:** When you compare your advantages and disadvantages with theirs, will you survive? Will you come out on top? How adaptable are they, and how adaptable are you? What can you do to minimize the risk from your competitors?

7. **New type of product:** Is there a market for it? Do you need to develop a market? Is consumer awareness high or low? Is your market segment motivated to buy? What steps will you take to overcome these problems?

8. **Liability:** What liability for you does your product or service incur? Are you liable for injuries or damage through its use? Could your employees cause damage or injury to customers, either in your shop or at the customer's location? Are you sufficiently insured? What toll on profits could warranty re-

pair or returns take? What can you do to specifically limit or eliminate these risks?

9. **Marketing risks:** Could marketing efforts be better timed? Is your market segment ill-defined? Have you fully analyzed your ad campaign and put your dollars where they do the most? Are you using tried-and-true techniques, or are you experimenting? Will your experimenting bankrupt you if it fails? Are your ads in any way libelous or false?

"RISKS" WORKSHEET

1. You:

2. Your family:

3. Your employees and partners:

4. Your finances:

5. Your markets:

6. Your competition:

7. New product risks:

8. Product, service, or employee liabilities:

9. Marketing risks:

(Work space)

Step Six

CREATE A "FINANCES" SECTION

MONEY IN, MONEY OUT

When you start any business, money flows out. Some time later, when your customers' checks start rolling in, you will hopefully find yourself making a profit over and above your expenses. Even though cash-flow is a difficult thing to predict, you must try. Lenders will want to see your financial projection for the next five years before loaning you money. How do you make these projections?

In the finances section of your business plan, you will break your financial situation down into several manageable parts. These can be roughly divided into a Personal Financial Statement, which examines your assets, liabilities and cash-flow, and a Business Financial Statement which shows how money flows out of your company, and how it flows in from your customers and other sources.

It is absolutely vital that you take into account all aspects of your cash flow and completely document everything. Lenders will look very closely at your assumptions, your research, and your facts and figures, so be prepared to back everything up with solid information.

CONTENTS OF "FINANCES"

Personal Financial Statement:

    Income — money coming in per month
    Debts — money going out per month
    Income After Expenses — income minus debts
    Assets — money and valuables which you own
    Liabilities — debts which you owe to others
    Net Worth — assets minus liabilities

Business Financial Statement:

Cost of Sales—how much of each sale is profit and how much is expense?

Operating Expenses—what does it cost per month to run your business?

Profit and Loss—how much will you make or lose each month?

Start-up Costs—how much will it cost to start your business?

Start-up Funds—how much money can you get from where to start your business?

EXAMPLES

LYCRA LAND CLOTHING

Personal Financial Statement—Income

Salary/Wages

The Derailleur Bicycle Shop	$52,000/yr.
The Gap Clothing Store	$ 5,400/yr.
	$57,400/yr

Money Owed Me

John Hones $4,000 2 years	$ 2,000/yr.
Steve Sanki $9,000 6 years	$ 1,500/yr.
	$ 3,500/yr.

Dividends/Interest

First Federal Savings and Loan	$ 450/yr.
First National Savings Bank	$ 273/yr.
IBM (30 shares)	$ 120/yr.
	$ 843/yr.

Property
    45 Alpine, Boulder, CO 80304 $ 7,500/yr.

    Total Annual Income $69,243/yr.

Personal Financial Statement
    — Depts Loans
        Chevy Chase Visa — MD $40/mo. $ 480/yr.
        American Express fee $ 60/yr.
        John Smith $120/mo. $ 1440/yr.
    Reals Estate
        Home Mortgage — $1,100/mo. $13,200/yr.
        Patte Valley Mortgage Co.
    Taxes
        Property tax $ 1,200/yr.
        Income Tax $ 5,320/yr.
    Insurance
        Auto $ 724/yr.
    Living Expenses
        Home/personal $19,000/yr.
    Other Expenses
        Child Support $10,000/yr.

    Total Annual Debts $51,424/yr.

Personal Financial Statement
    —Income After Expenses
        Total Annual Income $ 69,243
        Total Annual Debts   -$ 51,424

    Total Income After Expenses $ 17,819

Personal financial Statement — Assets
  Real Estate
    Residence: 45 Alpine , Boulder, CO $ 154,000
  Automobiles
    1991 Toyota Land Cruiser $ 19,560
    1985 Subaru Wagon $ 3,500
  Cash
    First National Bank $ 20,140
  Stocks
    IBM 30 shares $ 3,000
  Jewelry
    Family heirlooms $ 15,000
  Notes Receivable
    Loan to son, 8%, 3 years $ 7,000

Total Assets $222,200

Personal Financial Statement — Liabilities
  Credit Cards
    Revolving Visa Card $ 2,500
  Real Estate
    First deed of trust, $320/mo., 10.5%
    payable in 9 years $ 45,500
  Notes
    Auto — First National bank, $100/mo.,
    13% payable in 4 years $ 3,450

Total Liabilities $51,450
Personal Financial Statement — Net Worth
  Total Assets $222,200
  Total Liabilities   -$ 51,450

Net Worth $170,750

Business Financial Statement
  —Cost of Sales

Expected Sales		Cost/Sale	Total Cost of Sales
Body-wear	$145,000	50%	$ 72,500
Swimwear	$ 75,000	45%	$ 33,750
Accessories	$ 6,3000	35%	$ 6,300

Total	$238,000/yr.	47%	$112,550/yr.
	$ 19,833/mo.		$ 9,379/mo.

Business Financial Statemnet
  —Operating Expenses

Wages	$ 2,900/mo.
Benefits	$ 320/mo.
Rent	$ 2,400/mo.
Insurance	$ 145/mo.
Utilities	$ 375/mo.
Taxes	$ 67/mo.
Bookkeeping	$ 50/mo.
Depreciation	$ 50/mo.
Advertising	$ 1,000/mo.
Vehicles	$ 325/mo.
Loan Payments	$ 1,000/mo.

Total Monthly Operating Expenses	$ 9,632/mo.

Business Financial Statement
  —Profit and Loss

Total Sales Revenue	$ 19,833/mo.
Total Cost of Sales	-$ 9,379/mo.
Total Operating Expenses	-$ 9,632/mo.

Total Profit	$ 822/mo.

Business Financial Statement
    —Start-up Costs
        Inventory $ 14,000
        Equipment $ 8,000
        Marketing $ 1,000
        Lease, deposits, fees $ 3,500
                                         _____

    Total Start-up Costs $ 26,500

Business Financial Statement
    —Start-up Funds
        Personal Cash $ 14,000
        Bank Loan $ 14,000
                                         _____

    Total Start-up Funds $ 28,000

HOW TO WRITE YOUR OWN "FINANCES" SECTION

Personal Financial Statement

Personal Income

1. What are your current salary and wages? List all sources. Attach supporting pay statements.

2. What money is owed to you? List from whom, amount, terms. Attach copies of the loan agreements.

3. What is your dividend and interest income? List source and amount. Attach supporting documents.

4. What income do you have from property? List rental, lease and use fees. Attach supporting evidence.

5. What other sources of income do you have? List source and amount. Attach supporting evidence.

6. Add up #1-5 for your total personal income.

Personal Debts

7. What loans do you have outstanding? List lender, amount, terms. Attach copies of the loan agreements.

8. What real estate mortgages, rents, leases, or other costs are you paying? List to whom, amount. Attach copies of mortgage document.

9. What taxes are you paying? List all income, property and other taxes. Attach copies of last year's tax returns.

10. What insurance premiums are you paying? List health, auto, home and other premiums paid by you (not by your company), and not already included under real estate mortgages. Attach supporting evidence.

11. What are your living expenses? Include food, transport, clothing and all other day-to-day expenses.

12. What other expenses do you incur on a regular basis? List child support, college education, etc.

13. Add up #7-12 for your total debts.

Income after Expenses

14. Subtract your debts from your income.

Assets

15. What real estate do you own? List address, value. Attach copies of title, appraisal of value, and sales contract.

16. What automobiles do you own? List make, model, year, current blue-book value. Attach copies of your titles.

17. What cash assets do you have? List bank and amount. Attach photocopies of bank statements.

18. What stock, bonds or other savings do you have? List type, place, and amount. Attach supporting documents.

19. What other valuable assets do you have? List anything that banks could use as collateral against a loan, such as jewelry, boats, computers, cameras, etc. Attach appraisals or insurance forms as supporting evidence of value.

20. What notes receivable do you have? List loans to friends, outstanding debts owed to you, etc. Attach copies of the notes.

21. Add up # 15-20 for your total assets.

Liabilities

22. What credit card debts do you have? List card, amount, rate. Attach supporting documents, such as credit card bill photocopies.

23. What real estate debts do you have? List type, amount, terms. Attach mortgage contract photocopy.

24. What notes payable do you have? List lender, amount, and terms. Attach supporting photocopies of agreements.

25. What other liabilities do you have? Attach supporting documents.

26. Add up #22-25 for your total liabilities.

Net Worth

27. Subtract your liabilities from your assets for your net worth.

Business Financial Statement

Cost of Sales

28. What are your expected sales revenues, percent spent on each sale, and total cost of sales? The total cost per sale on the bottom line of the example is calculated by dividing your total cost of sales by your total expected sales revenues. Attach supporting documents, market studies, competition studies, etc.

29. What are your operating expenses? Include wages (including your own), benefits paid,

rent, insurance, utilities, taxes, bookkeeping (CPA fees, for example), depreciation of equipment, advertising costs, vehicle costs and any other regular business expenses. Attach supporting documents.

30. What is your profit or loss? Start with your total sales revenues and subtract total sales costs and operating expenses to determine your profit or loss.

31. What are your start-up costs? Include all one-time purchases of inventory, equipment, marketing costs, leases, deposits, business fees, and other start-up expenses. Attach supporting documents.

32. What start-up funds do you need? List amounts and where you will get them. Generally lenders will require you to come up with 50 percent of the funds for your new business, so that you have as much to lose as they have.

"FINANCES" WORKSHEET

Personal Financial Statement

Personal Income

1. Salary, wages:

2. Money owed to you:

3. Dividend, interest income:

4. Real estate income:

5. Other sources of income:

6. TOTAL PERSONAL INCOME:

Personal Debts

7. Outstanding loans:

8. Real estate mortgages, rents, leases:

9. Taxes:

10. Insurance premiums:

11. Living expenses:

12. Other expenses:

13. TOTAL PERSONAL DEBTS:

14. INCOME AFTER EXPENSES:

Personal Assets

15. Real estate:

16. Automobiles:

17. Cash:

18. Stocks, bonds, etc:

19. Other assets:

20. Notes receivable:

21. TOTAL ASSETS

Personal Liabilities

22. Credit cards:

23. Real estate debts:

24. Notes payable by you:

25. Other liabilities:

26. TOTAL LIABILITIES:

27. NET WORTH:

Business Financial Statement

Cost of Sales
28. Sales revenues, % cost of sales, total cost of sales:

29. Operating expenses:

30. Profit or loss:

31. Start-up costs:

32. Start-up funds needed:

(Work space)

CREATE "MILESTONES" AND "THE COMPANY" SECTIONS

MAPPING THE FUTURE

You have done a lot of work so far. You know what you are going to sell, to whom, who your competition is, how you will make your product, how you will market it, what the risks are, and what kind of finances will be involved.

The next question is *when*.

We have all probably seem "time-lines" at some point in our education. They lay out events in history so that it is easy to see what occurred when. The milestones section of your business plan is very much the same thing. It lays out what major events and goals are important to your company in the next five years, and when each should be achieved.

Your potential lender can determine from the previous sections of your plan what your new business will do, but not when. With the milestones section, he can grasp your time frame of operations.

You also can use the milestones section to plan for events, such as the purchase of equipment, the hiring of more employees, seasonal highs and lows, and even vacations. When you enter into the start-up phase and begin purchasing equipment and readying your shop, you will have a daunting number of tasks to take care of. You can expand the Milestones section to include all these tasks, turning it into a daily or weekly schedule.

CONTENTS OF "MILESTONES"

Milestones begins as a simple list of important events and dates. However, to be accurate in your dates, you must do some hard thinking. Perhaps you need to buy a large piece of equipment. That is a milestone in your list. However, since it will be expensive, you decide to plan ahead to come up with the necessary cash by holding a series of summer sales. These are also events. To hold the sales, you must pre-order your stock — more events.

It is easy to get bogged down in detail! The key to your milestones section right now is to put down major events only. These should include such things as space-rental, hiring, inventory ordering and arrival, opening day, break-even date, loan-pay-off date, and so on.

Later, once you are beginning to spend money on start-up, you may want to begin adding detail to your milestones section, to make it a working schedule of things to do and to prepare for. For now, however, stick to events which hold major significance for you and your lenders and partners.

EXAMPLE

LYCRA LAND

October 1	Loans secured
October 5	Store equipment ordered
October 6	Newspaper ads booked for Nov. 3
October 7	Store decorators booked.
October 8	Fliers created for University distrib.
October 15	Store lease begins
October 16	Inventory ordered
October 16	Store decoration begins
October 17	Employee interviews begin
October 24	Store decoration finishes
October 24	Inventory begins arriving
October 25	Equipment begins arriving
November 4	Opening day.

HOW TO WRITE YOUR OWN "MILESTONES" SECTION

1. *What are the major events which must happen before opening day?*

Include financial, personal, business, and all other major events.

2. *What major events do you expect in the first three "shakedown" months?*

These might include employee training, sales, ad campaigns, and financial events.

3. *What major events can you predict for the first five years?*

Think about your product, production, markets, marketing, competition, and finances.

4. *In what order must events happen?*

For example, you must decorate a store (paint, carpet, etc.) before you move in equipment, and you must have your shelves and racks in place before moving in the inventory. Go through your lists of events above and prioritize their occurrence. Think about interdependencies.

"MILESTONES" WORKSHEET

1. Pre-opening events:

2. Events in the first 3 months:

3. Events in the first five years:

(Work space)

HISTORY, PEOPLE, AND THE ORGANIZATION

The first, and often the only, aspects of your business which most people will see is that your business produces, markets, and sells some product or service. Customers, lenders, and others who are not intimately involved in the operational details need to have a better feel for the inner workings of your organization.

The company section of your business plan describes in some detail the history of the company, its key players, its goals and its management. Lenders in particular will want to know where a company has been (if you are buying or taking over an existing company) and where it is going. What is the company's strategy?

CONTENTS OF "THE COMPANY"

History:

This part gives a brief overview of the history of the company, how and when it was created, by whom, and what its goals were. It also looks at the growth and significant historical events of the company.

Status:

A look at the current state of the company, both financially, managerially, and in employees, facilities, profits, sales, and other ways.

Goals:

This part examines where the company is headed, and what its future goals are. Whether it is a high-growth entrepreneurial firm, or a stable service-oriented business, lenders and others will want a summary of what course you intend to sail.

Players:

Personalities are often vital to the success of a company. The key players are you, your partners, and any other people of major importance in the direction, skills, or financing of the company.

Management:

The management style of a company is also important. Will it be a rigidly structured research-and-development environment, or will it be a free-floating "deal with it when it happens" style?

EXAMPLE

CONTINENTAL CUISINE CATERING

Continental Cuisine was created in 1991 to serve the Longmont community by exploiting needs for catering in the local market. It offers a variety of European cuisines, cooked to order largely at each customer's event.

The company's immediate goals are to achieve start-up by January 15th, in time to book its services for the lucrative spring wedding season. It will start with seven employees and a main shop and kitchen located

on Main Street, and eventually expand to twelve employees in the course of one year. Market research has determined that Continental Cuisine should gross $100,000 or more in its first year.

Long-term goals include geographical expansion of service into the surrounding communities, and into nearby Boulder as well. Though focusing primarily on residential customers, Continental Cuisine will at six months begin exploring the booming corporate markets as well, using standard trial marketing techniques.

John Sullivan, owner and founder, is the driving force behind the creation of Continental Cuisine. His long experience as a chef for New York's Stanwich Hotels, and later as catering manager for the small but prestigious company La Pluma, bring over twelve years of industry experience to the company. He has settled permanently now in Longmont, and will be working full-time for the creation, management, and success of Continental Cuisine.

Based on his experience in New York, Sullivan plans to manage the seven employees with a flexible, "as needed" style. "Happy employees are vital to the success of each catering job, especially since their attitudes have a great deal to do with the emotional success of catered events. Thus, Continental Cuisine will adopt a liberal policy regarding scheduling and personal time off, while at the

same time maintaining high standards of skill, conduct, and dress."

The company is in the process of securing $35,000 in start-up financing, 50 percent from Sullivan's private sources, and 50 percent from a ten-year, 13-percent interest bank loan.

HOW TO WRITE YOUR OWN "THE COMPANY" SECTION

1. What is the history of your company?

Include when it was created, by whom, what were its goals, and what were major milestones in the history of the company.

2. What is the current state of the company?

Include size, facilities, employees (skills, wages, benefits), financial state, sales, achievements, and problems. Is it a high growth-oriented company, or a stable slow-grower?

3. What are the immediate and future goals of the company?

These could be financial, expansion, survival, restructuring, new products or services, the elimination of certain unprofitable products and services, or even a change in leadership.

4. Who are the key players in the company?

Include yourself, partners, financial supporters, employees with vital technical skills, and any other movers and shakers vital to the organization. Describe their experience and what they bring to the company. You may want to attach a copy of your resume to this section.

5. How is the company structured and managed?

Describe the management of the company, flow of control, decision making process, and so on. These aspects can be very important in partnerships, where disagreements on decision making can lead to disaster, and in larger companies where unclear flow of control can create fatal chaos.

"THE COMPANY" WORKSHEET

1. History:

2. Current state:

3. Immediate and future goals:

4. Key players:

5. Structure:

(Work space)

Step Eight

CREATE A "SUMMARY" SECTION

AN OVERVIEW OF YOUR COMPANY

The summary, often referred to as the executive summary, is a short synopsis of your whole company. It briefly summarizes all the information in the sections you have just completed: the product, market, competition, production, marketing, financials, and management. It is the single most important section of your plan. It forms your readers' first impressions of you and your business. And it is brief!

Why? Most people who read your business plan will be busy with little time to waste. Bankers and other lenders will want to know what your company does, and whether it is economically viable. Potential business partners will want to get a feel for the company quickly to judge whether it is a good place in which to invest their time, energy, and money. Possible new employees will want to know if your business fits with their career goals, their interests, and their skills. In each case, these busy people need a quick overview of your new company. The summary gives them this.

Once readers have seen the summary, they will probably have many specific questions for you. The other more detailed sections of your business plan can then help answer these questions. Reading the summary is similar to meeting a person for the first time. The reader forms an immediate impression of your company. And as you know, first impressions are made once, and they often last a long, long time. What kind of first impressions should your summary make? Professional. Well thought-out. Concise. Brief. Accurate. Interesting. Successful.

Let's take a look at the specifics.

CONTENTS OF A "SUMMARY"

The summary contains material drawn from all of the sections of your business plan written in Step One through Step Seven. The summary contains a brief description of:

1. Opportunity and goal.
2. The name of your company and a brief history of it and its key players (owner, manager, etc.).
3. Products or services the company produces, and what market needs these fill.
4. Markets.
5. Competition.
6. Marketing.
7. Your company's current composition.
8. Your company's current financial state, future prospects.
9. How much money is needed and for what.
10. Future milestones.

EXAMPLE

LYCRA LAND CLOTHING

More of America's general populace plays sports than that of any other country. And Boulder, Colorado, dubbed America's Number One Sporting Town by *Outside* Magazine, leads the growing health and fitness trend. Its 300 days of sunshine per year, its moun-

tains, and the high altitude have drawn cyclists, runners, and other athletes from around the USA and the world. Over 50 percent of its population of 60,000 residents and 24,000 university students indulge in some sort of outdoor sports.

Lycra Land, a body- and swimwear retailer, plans to exploit this large and growing market by opening a 1,200 square foot store in the heart of Boulder's well-loved and heavily traversed Pearl Street Pedestrian Mall. Its market segment includes the estimated 16,000 physically active university students, most of whom are upper middle class, and the 30,000 active residents whose mean income is $35,000 per year.

Lycra Land's competition includes six general-inventory sporting-goods stores and five retail clothing stores in Crossroads Mall. Its advantages are an excellent location and a larger selection of strictly body- and swimwear than is offered by its competitors.

The main marketing thrust will be two-fold. A dynamic and energetic shop window display of models "in-action" on snow boards, mountain bikes, and other gear will attract sporting people from the Pearl Street Mall; and an advertising campaign in local newspapers and on cable television's CNN and MTV channels will be aimed at University of Colorado students and at active working-residents between 20 and 45 years old.

The company was founded in 1991 by Anita Sutherland, who has recently spent three years as a clothing store manager for Close Encounters of Denver, where she designed and implemented an extremely successful marketing campaign. She worked the previous seven years as a retail sales-person at various other clothing stores in the Denver metro area, and so brings ten years of accumulated business knowledge and marketing innovation to Lycra Land.

Currently Sutherland has raised $14,000 in start-up funds from personal sources, and is seeking an additional $14,000 in loans to start this sole-proprietorship. Major costs include shop-rent, remodeling, equipment, inventory, and marketing, which total $26,500. Projected sales during the first three months, based on market and competition studies, should average close to $20,000 per month. Total operating expenses and costs of sales will leave a profit of approximately $822 per month, which will be reinvested into the business.

Opening day is planned for March 15, 1991. Break-even should occur within one month of opening according to market and profitability studies performed by Wilson & Shares Consultants. Loan pay-off can be achieved by March, 1995. While Lycra Land has the potential for high-growth in the current local market, the first three years will be largely dedicated to achieving company financial stability and a solid market-share.

HOW TO WRITE YOUR OWN "SUMMARY" SECTION

Your goals in writing the summary are:

1. Inform readers about the nature of your idea.

2. Excite readers to share in your opportunity.

3. Convince readers of your idea's viability.

As in previous sections, the following steps are only a guide. You may find that certain information is unimportant in your situation and opt to omit it. Other information may be very important and may need more space for clarification.

Throughout the following steps, always keep in mind one question: What is really important for your readers to know about your company?

1. Opportunity and Goal:

You have seen some opportunity and you are planning to do something (or you wouldn't be writing this business plan). What is the opportunity you plan to exploit? (A new location, a change in the marketplace, a better product, an unfilled niche, etc.) How long will that opportunity last? (A new location opening up might be snapped up very quickly, while a new market niche for a state-of-the-art widget might last years or decades.)

How will the opportunity grow or shrink with time? (A new car-wash for example is dependent on the population of the area. If the town is rapidly growing, the opportunity is growing. If the town is having hard times and people are moving out, the opportunity is shrinking.)

What are your goals in view of this opportunity? What specific scheme will you use to exploit the opportunity? (Start a new business, buy, expand or tighten up an existing business, etc.)

2. Company Name, History, Key Players:

Introduce your company to your readers. This is remarkably like introducing a friend whom you know well to someone.

What is your company called, and when was it or will it be founded? Is it a sole proprietorship, a partnership, or incorporated? What are some key events in its past (if it is an existing company)? (Growth, changes of ownership, changes of location, successes and other events.)

Who are the key players? (You, owner, manager, and any other important brains or backers. Don't mention employees who are not vital players in the big picture.) What do these people bring to the company? (Direction, money, time/energy, technical knowledge, etc.)

3. Products, Services, Market-Needs:

What your company produces and why there is a need for these products or services.

What does your company produce? (Products, services, delivery, communications, etc.) What market-need does your product fill? Does the need exist, or must you artificially create the need?

4. Your Markets:

What slice of the population you will sell your product to, and what in particular distinguishes them from everyone else. This is often referred to as your "market segment."

Who are your markets geographically? Economically? In age? Socially? In groups?

Are your markets accessible? Through what mechanism?

Will your markets accept your product? Why?

5. Competition:

Your competition in your chosen market segments. This is a very important section. If you omit it from your plan, lenders and others will conclude that you have not researched your idea sufficiently.

Who are your current competitors? (Locally, nationally, internationally.) Who can you expect your future competitors to be? (If you are onto a good thing, you will soon have competitors.)

What is their share of the existing market? (If a small town already has seven pizza parlors, they have the market pretty well sewn up, and your chances are dim. If, however, you're the only Chinese Carry Out in town, you have a much larger share of the dinner-delivery market.)

What edge does your competition have over you? (Size, long standing in the community, cable TV advertising, better product.)

6. Your Edge Over the Competition:

What your business will do to gain its share of the market from existing and future competition.

What technical edge do you have? (A better widget, higher quality, more or better features, ease of use.) What cost edge do you have? (Cheaper production methods, cheaper raw materials, cheaper labor.) What time edge do you have? (Faster delivery, easier ordering such as an 800 number, quick customized production.)

What sales and marketing edge do you have? (Using an existing customer base from some other business, using sophisticated advertising, using mailing lists, using a new or better strategy than your competition.)

What other edges do you possess or will you develop?

7. Company's Composition:

What your company physically consists of.

What facilities do you/will you have? (A shop, office, kitchen, warehouse, etc.)

What equipment do you/will you have? (production equipment, delivery equipment, vehicle, managerial equipment, etc.)

How many people do you/will you employ?

8. Financial State and Future Prospects:

Current finances, income and debts, future income and debts.

What financial resources do you and your company have now? (cash available, bank loans, partnerships, personal, sales of assets, etc.) What are the business's current income, its payments, and its debts?

What changes in income, payments, and debts are anticipated? (Higher profits, lower production costs, paying off old vehicle, buying second vehicle, etc.)

9. Money Needed:

Additional financial resources you will need in the next two years. (What you are asking banks or other lenders for.)

How much money will you need? And what for? (Include expansion, debts, relocation, new equipment, remodeling, and any other needs in this prediction.) Will you need it all at once? Can you spread it out? (You might need a lump sum to close on a building. You might need a series of smaller loans to buy new equipment for a phased-expansion.)

What kind of pay-back schedule do you need? (one-, five- thirty-year loans.) How do your anticipated profits let you achieve the payback schedule? (Very important to lenders. Can you realistically pay them back with interest, or will you go belly up?)

10. Milestones:

Major events anticipated in the future, and their predicted dates. (This section is an easy-to-read checklist of events showing where the company is headed.)

"SUMMARY" WORKSHEET

Opportunity and goal:

Company name, history, key players:

Products, services, and market-needs for them:

Markets:

Competition:

Your advantage over the competition:

Composition of company:

Financial state and future prospects:

Money needed:

Major milestones:

(Work space)

Step Nine

CREATE YOUR FINAL BUSINESS PLAN

The hard work of creating your business plan is done. As with any professional document, its appearance will affect how lenders and others react to it. A professional look and feel further increase your chances of getting your loan. So, now it is time to add a few final details, put the final polish on the plan, and have it typed and printed.

CREATE A TITLE PAGE

The title page is straightforward, presenting the name and address of your company:

BUSINESS PLAN

for

LYCRA LAND CLOTHING STORE

January 21, 1992
Submitted by:
Anita Sutherland
1234 Spruce Street
Boulder, Colorado 81234
(303) 444-4321

CREATE A TABLE OF CONTENTS

We have until now examined the various sections of your business plan in the order in which it is easiest for you to create your plan. Now you will re-order the sections into the proper format for presentation. At this point you prob-

ably have pages of notes and many photocopied supporting documents. Take all of your notes, charts, financial
statements, and other materials and place them in the
order shown below.

The table of contents helps lenders and others quickly
flip through your business plan to find sections of interest
to them, just like the table of contents of a book. You should
write down your table of contents entries first. Then, when
you have your document typed on a computer, the word
processor can automatically assign the proper page numbers. If you hand-type it on a typewriter, type the table of
contents last after all of the page numbers in the document
have been assigned. The final result looks like this:

Table of Contents

Remember when you are numbering your pages (or
having the word processor do it) to leave blank pages
where you will insert your photocopied attachments, those

supporting documents such as market analysis, bank statements, mortgage contracts, and so on.

POLISH YOUR ROUGH DRAFT

Now that you have all of your notes ready and organized, it is time to put it all aside for a day or two. Go fishing, play with the kids, go out to dinner and a movie. Take a break and cool your brain cells. Every good writer learns that by shelving it for a couple of days, he can return to it with a fresh eye. Mistakes are much easier to spot, omissions leap out, and corrections become obvious.

After your break, read through your rough draft and supporting documents. In each section of your business plan, ask yourself the following questions:

1. What basic information have I left out?

2. What questions could my lender ask me about this section that I have not answered?

3. Are all my claims accurate?

4. Are all my facts and figures accurate?

5. What supporting material is missing?

6. What supporting material is shaky?

7. Does the text read well?

8. Are all of my statements consistent?

9. Do all my goals, analysis and strategies make sense?

10. Is this plan convincing?

If you have any doubts, rewrite the section, add the missing information, and check your facts. Remember, unlike school where you simply got graded on your accuracy, your own hard-earned cash is now at stake. While inaccuracies and unsubstantiated facts may slip by your loan examiner, they could do you damage later.

HAVE YOUR BUSINESS PLAN PRINTED

Word processing services have popped up in virtually every city in the nation. You should be able to find one easily. One important reason for using a "WP" service is that a document printed on a laser printer and then neatly bound looks professional and presents you and your company in a professional manner. First impressions are important.

A second reason to use a WP service is that you will find your business plan useful as your business grows. It will be a living, breathing document which will help you for as long as you own your business, and even if and when you decide to sell it. An up-to-date plan is very useful, while an unmaintained, obsolete plan does little good. So you will want to make changes and additions to your business plan. Virtually all WP services store your document on a computer diskette, which you can take home with you. Later, when you want to make revisions to the plan, you just bring the diskette to the WP service, and they can quickly make changes and additions without retyping the whole document. This saves you both time and a considerable amount of money.

Here is a checklist of questions to ask when you shop around for a word processing service:

1. Do you use a laser printer? (Laser printers give the best results, while dot-matrix and other printer output is inferior.)

2. Can you automatically number pages? (They should.)

3. Can you generate a table of contents with page numbers? (They should be able to do this automatically.)

4. Can you spell-check the document? (They should.)

5. What will you charge for creating this document? (Usually charges are hourly or page-rates.)

6. When can you have it done?

7. Can I see samples of your work? (Check the quality with a critical eye.)

Comparison shop as many WP services as possibly. Rates vary considerably, as does the quality of service.

HAVE PROFESSIONALS REVIEW YOUR PLAN

No matter how much you have labored over your plan, it is still good to have it reviewed by another pair of eyes. Professional consultants, such as CPAs versed in small business practices, are relatively inexpensive, and can offer important advice, and spot potentially fatal mistakes.

When you shop around for a consultant, check CPAs, banks which deal with small business loans regularly, and try calling the local branch of the Small Business Administration (SBA). The SBA sponsors the Service Corps of Retired Executives (SCORE), who are often a good source of experience.

Your consultant should have several years experience owning or operating a small business, should be a professional, and should be interested in working with you on your plan. Have him look over your plan and make notes on it about your basic assumptions, the plan's content, presentation, and any other factors which may be lacking.

Finally, after having your plan reviewed, make the appropriate changes and have another final draft printed. Remember that a consultant's suggestions are just that: suggestions. You, not he, will have to present your plan to the loan officer, and you, not he, will have to lay your money down, so you should critically examine his advice.

Once you have made the final revisions, make one copy of the plan for each lender you intend to approach. They will want to hold on to your business plan while they review your loan. You should also make a copy for yourself, and about three extras. Number the copies so that you can keep track of them. Also, don't hand out copies indiscriminately — show them only to people who need to know. Business strategies and plans which could be potentially damaging to your competitors (and good for you) should be kept secret from all who don't need to know.

USING YOUR BUSINESS PLAN

ASKING FOR MONEY

It is time to obtain money for your new business, and now is when all your hard work on your business plan will pay off. Asking for money is sometimes an intimidating process to the uninitiated. The prospect of someone in a gray business suit behind a large oak desk poring over all your debts, your bank accounts, and asking personal questions about your credit card bills, may not seem a pleasant prospect. However, keep one very important fact in mind throughout this process: Lenders want to loan you money! That is their business and that is how they put bread on their table. All they really desire in the end is to be sure that you can pay back the loan and that they are guaranteed a profit on it.

When you put down the final amount that you want to borrow, don't be afraid to ask for ample funds. Many new businesses with good ideas and plans fail because they are under-capitalized. It is vital to have enough money on hand to buy equipment, obtain work-space, pay salaries, and cover unexpected costs. The Small Business Administration recommends that you also have enough working capital to carry you and the business through a full three months. So ask for all that you need.

All lenders commonly look for several things in both you and your business. Not surprisingly, you will recognize them all. In the next section we will examine what lenders want to see before they approve a loan, how to write and support your loan application, and how to use your business plan and other documents when you walk into the lender's office.

There are many different kinds of places to get money. In addition to banks, you should think about other sources which may be more cost-effective for your particular needs. Some may charge lower interest, and some may not charge any interest at all. We will examine a variety of places you can look in Sources of Money later in this chapter.

WHAT LENDERS LOOK FOR

Every lender wants to answer one very basic question before he approves a loan for your new business: Can you pay back the loan and interest as planned? He wants his money back on schedule, and he wants to make a profit on it.

In order to answer that fundamental question, lenders ask a lot of other more detailed questions. You will soon use your business plan and loan application to answer his detailed questions to his satisfaction. If you have followed the steps in this manual, thought carefully about your new business, have planned well, and have written a good business plan, you will almost certainly get the loan you need. Let's take a look at the standard questions any lender will ask:

- What kind of credit rating do you and your company have? If you are asking for a loan for an existing company, lenders will examine its financial history. Is the company making money? Does it have dry seasons? What are its debts? Can it cover all expenses including the cost of the loan and still turn a profit? If you are starting a new company, the lender will have to rely on the credit ratings of you and any other key backers. Your business plans Finances section should contain information which supports your credit rating. The lender will want to see:

Your Assets — cash, stocks, bonds, real estate, cash-value insurance policies, personal property, debts owed to you, deeds, and mortgages or trusts owed to you. The more assets you have, the better, since lenders can often attach your assets if you default on their loan.

Your liabilities — all loans, mortgage payments, credit card accounts, etc. The less liabilities you currently have, the better. If you can show that you have successfully paid off past liabilities, however, your credit rating improves.

Your net worth — your total assets minus your total liabilities. The higher the better.

- How will this loan be used to help your company? The loan should be a positive step for your business. A positive step means that the use of the loan will increase the net worth or viability of the company in some way, after taking into account the cost (interest) of the loan. A second delivery truck with which to reach more customers might be a worthwhile benefit to your business. A new Jaguar XJE sports car for your personal use is probably not, unless you can come up with a very, very inventive justification! So, be prepared to show how the loan will be of benefit, by using some combination of the goals, finances, and milestones set down in your business plan. [Summary, The Company, and other sections.]

- Can you repay the loan before its value is exhausted? If you take out a loan for a delivery truck which can realistically be expected to last four years under heavy business use, the term of the loan should be no longer than four years. If you are still paying the loan when the truck has become scrap metal, you have dug yourself into a hole. [Finances section.]

- How is your product or service accepted in the marketplace? If you make widgets, you must have a reliable set of customers who will buy and keep on buying your widgets. You must be able to reach these markets, motivate them to buy your widgets, and they must be able to afford the cost of your widgets. [Products/Services and Markets sections.]

- Does your product benefit your customers? The product must benefit the customer in some way. Benefits include the obvious (eat it, drive it, make something with it), and the more sublime (make the customer feel good, enhance sex appeal, reduce stress). If the product is of no benefit in any way, it won't sell, and you won't get your loan. [Products section.]

- Who is your competition and how do your products compare? Even if you currently do not have competition, the fact that you are on to a good idea will encourage others to try your idea, too. Success generates competition. If you have not analyzed your competition, the lender will conclude that you are operating in dream-land, and won't give you a loan. [Competition section.]

- What edge do you have over your competition, and what edge do they have over you? Lenders always examine the competition to try to determine your chances of success in your real-world, hard-knocks marketplace. They want to understand what your advantages are, and what the competition's advantages are. Is your competition going to rub your face in the dirt and make you cry "Chapter 11"? [Competition section.]

- How do you market your product? Lenders want to be assured that you have good markets (your market segment), that you can reach them effectively (your marketing strategy), and that these customers will buy your product. If you can't reach and motivate your customers, you can't make a profit or pay off the loan. [Markets section.]

- Are your facts, figures, timetable, and predictions realistic? Your projected profit and loss figures must be based on solid facts which take into account all the variables of the business. Your timetable should take into account that your employees, suppliers, contractors, and you are all human beings, not supermen. Things take time; be realistic. Your predictions of market conditions, new competition, and other factors should be based on as much solid evidence as you can gather. Lenders are not impressed by the Ouija-board schedules. Remember, if the lender uncovers one bogus "guesstimate" in your data, he will wonder if all your "facts" are that unreliable. So, if your data has a margin for error, state it. [All sections.]

- Is the loan large enough? This might seem to be an odd question, but it is a fact that many new businesses collapse because they are under-funded. Don't be afraid to ask for as much money as you really need. The lender would much rather give you a larger loan (and make more interest) if it insures the success of your business (and your ability to pay him back). Too little money, especially in a start-up situation, can be deadly to a new business. The SBA recommends that your start-up capital should be large enough to carry you and your business through three full months.

SOURCES OF MONEY

When you see the word "loan" you probably get a mental image of the bank down the road. True, banks do give loans. But there are many other sources of working capital, some of which might just be a more sensible deal for your particular situation.

First, read through the following list, and see which sources of money might be available to you. Second, analyze the pros and cons of each source before you make your decision on which ones to approach, and prioritize them. You may want to use several different sources to spread your liability around. Let's take a look at some sources of money, and some easy ways to avoid spending it.

Personal Savings:

Advantages. The interest on your savings account which you lose when you withdraw the money will be less than the interest you would have to pay on most commercial (bank) loans, so it is cheaper. You have no payback schedule to meet. The money is available as you need it, a bit at a time or all at once.

Disadvantages. Your personal savings are a buffer against the unexpected, such as medical bills, car problems, or excessive Christmas shopping. You should always have enough in the bank to cover routine and unexpected emergencies. If you withdraw too much cash to use for your business, you may be compromising the personal security of you and your family.

Advice. Use savings when possible, but leave plenty of money in the bank to fall back on for personal emergencies.

Your House:

Advantages. You may be able to bring in hard cash quickly by refinancing your home or selling your property. You may also be able to get rid of a bad liability if the house is a money-sink, or if its value is depreciating rapidly.

Disadvantages. If you live in a high growth area, such as around Washington D.C., the longer you hold on to your house or property and let it appreciate the more you stand to make in the long run. Selling property now could cost you lots of potential earnings in the future.

Advice. Weigh the appreciation benefits over the time period you plan to own the property against the need to sell it for immediate cash. Check the current mortgage rates against what you are paying. If the current rates are two points or more lower than the rate you are paying, refinancing is probably cost effective. If the property is not appreciating well, and/or if it is not needed, consider selling it.

Friends:

Advantages. Friends might cut you a deal where you pay them interest on their loan where the rate is more than they can earn in savings, but less than other loan sources would charge you. Both people come out ahead. Payback terms are often more flexible than those of commercial lenders. Friends may also give you a loan in return for "a piece of the action."

Disadvantages. Many friendships have been ruined when the lender wants his money back early, or the borrower fails in his payment schedule. Emotions tend to be much more of a factor with this type of loan than with a bank. Your friend's "piece of the action" could be the demise of your business.

Advice. In spite of the fact that the lender is your friend, conduct the loan purely as a business deal. First, make sure that the loan doesn't put your friend into a financially precarious position. Then draw up a legal contract (it doesn't have to be particularly complicated) so that both parties know exactly what is expected and when. Clear, written communication is just as important here as when you are dealing with a bank.

Gifts:

Advantages. Gifts of money, land, vehicles, or other items of value from relatives or friends are perhaps the best source of money of all. You may not have to pay them back, or might be asked to pay them back "whenever," and you probably won't have to pay interest. You may not have to pay taxes on the gift — check with your CPA.

Disadvantages. The giver must be able to afford the gift. If they ask for it back later, they can put both you and them in bad straits if you have invested the money in your business. Be sure that there are no hidden strings, legal, emotional, or otherwise. This is business.

Advice. Make sure that the giver can afford the gift, and that both parties understand if, when and how much of it is to be paid back. And just because they are giving a gift, don't assume they are not interested in your business plan. Show them. It will greatly help to emotionally support them in their decision.

Partners:

Advantages. One or more partners can bring money, energy, time, and other assets to help your business get started and to grow. Debt liability can be split between partners, lessening the chances of each partner losing his shirt financially. Additional minds can bring new insights and ideas to the business. If one partner gets sick, the others can take up the slack and keep the business rolling.

Disadvantages. You are no longer the sole proprietor. Control, decision making, and the division of labor become more complicated. Friendships can be split up because of disagreements about how things should be done, about goals, and even over trivial details. Disagreements can lead to the demise of the business when one partner pulls out.

Advice. Investigate potential partners very carefully in every respect, from finances, to personality, to business approach. Then make sure in writing that each partner knows exactly what his responsibilities, limits, and bene-fits are, financially and otherwise. Try to install checks and balances so that partners doing their jobs properly have leverage against partners who are slacking off or violating the terms of the agreement. Think out and agree on how decisions will be made in advance. Preplan duties, relationships, and benefits in writing in advance.

Banks:

Advantages. Banks regularly lend start-up money to new businesses. Their loans generally cost you less than loans from other commercial sources such as mortgage brokers. They may lend you up to half of your needed cash.

Disadvantages. You must have a well thought-out business plan which can convince them that you can repay their loan as planned. They will only generally lend you half of the money you need, or less, expecting you to come up with the rest from your own private sources; the theory here is that you are more likely to succeed if you personally have a lot to lose. Banks require collateral — objects of value, such as your house or car — to which you give them title for the duration of the loan. If you fail to pay the loan, they keep and sell off the items of collateral.

Advice. Comparison shop by checking out loans from a number of different banks. Compare specifics: interest rate (often prime rate plus 3 percent), repayment schedule (you might be able to pay small amounts back for a while, then follow up with a big lump sum once your business is on its feet), whether you can pay back the loan faster than planned and save yourself interest, how the interest is paid off compared with how the principal is paid off (mostly interest at first?), and any other terms. Now compare the terms from different lenders against your business's financial expectations. Will you have a lot of cash coming in all at once a year from now? Or will you need to pay back the loan very gradually? Are you buying all your equipment at once, or investing piece by piece over the next couple of years? There is no "best" type of loan; there is only "best in your circumstances."

Stock:

Advantages. By selling stock to the public, you can raise large amounts of money. The Securities and Exchange Commission's S-18 form allows you to offer up to $7,500,000 in shares to the public. The federal government regulation D allows small businesses to skip much of the paperwork and other hassles normally associated with selling stock under certain conditions.

Disadvantages. There is still lots of paperwork. Expect large amounts of time and energy to be consumed by the mechanics of selling stock. Remember that when others own shares in your company, you are no longer the sole captain of your ship.

Advice. Sell stock when you need hundreds of thousands or millions of dollars. The hassles involved aren't often justified for small dollar amounts. Read the SEC Form S-18, and Regulations A and D, then talk to an expert. A variety of caps on the amount of stock you can offer exist, each with their own requirements and obligations. Determine what federal and state exemptions apply to your situation to reduce your burdens.

Venture Capital:

Advantages. By selling shares of your company to either large or small venture capitalists, you can raise large amounts of money quickly. Large "professional" venture capitalists are interested in quick and high return businesses. Small venture capitalists, such as friends, relatives or other "local people" are more flexible in the type of business they will fund, but still desire a high rate of return.

Disadvantages. Venture capitalists usually expect a large return on their investment quickly. Large venture capitalists deal mostly with high-tech, medical, or other high-return businesses. Giving up a large percentage (40 to 60 percent) of your profits to pay off venture capitalists can be very hard on your company during the start-up years. You are also bound by state securities laws, and must register all venture capital (securities) arrangements.

Advice. For a new, small business, contact friends and acquaintances to find interested investors. Once again, write contracts thoroughly and register them with the state, even if they are among friends or relatives. You must do this to be legal.

The Small Business Administration:

Advantages. The SBA is a government organization which specializes in helping new businesses start and succeed. It regularly makes loans to new businesses, or guarantees up to $500,000 in bank loans for 90 percent of the loan. Banks like SBA loans because they can collect their commission and then sell the loan on the open market easily. Loans are usually approved in two to four months.

Disadvantages. You will probably be asked to show that you cannot obtain all the needed money elsewhere, and why. This means that you must try alternative lenders first. You should have your loan application written by someone familiar with the machinations and rules of the SBA to be successful.

Advice. Try alternative lenders first. Have your SBA loan application professionally prepared by an organization familiar with the SBA (ask your local banks to recommend someone). Study the government instructions on SBA loans — these are often available at your local library as well as through SBA offices.

A Small Business Investment Company:

Advantages. SBICs take loans from the SBA and redistribute them to businesses, taking a profit. Minority Business Investment Companies (MBICs) also exist to help ethnic minority businesses get loans.

Disadvantages. SBICs take a cut off the top, which means you will probably pay more for your loan than if you went directly to the SBA.

Advice. Contact your local SBA office for the names and addresses of some of the nearest of the 400 SBICs. Comparison shop.

FmHA Loans:

Advantages. The Farmer's Home Administration guarantees bank loans in towns with small populations (50,000 or under) or low population densities (100 people per square mile or less). While FmHA doesn't itself lend money, its guarantees make banks much more willing to lend to you.

Disadvantages. FmHA guaranteed loans are slow, and may not apply in your geographical area.

Advice. Allow several months for the loan to be processed — the wheels turn slowly. To contact FmHA, look under U.S. Government, Department of Agriculture in the phone book.

Local or State Programs:

Advice. Towns and states have a huge variety of assistance programs for small business owners. To find these programs call your local Chamber of Commerce. Again, comparison shop!

Start Small:

Advantages. One obvious way to keep more money in the pot is not to spend it. How can you start your business with less cash? Many corporations have been started in a home garage instead of a "professional" location. (Apple Computer is a great example.) Some items can be bought used, or leased, or rented temporarily. Relatives might give you free shop labor for a while to help you get off the ground. Determine which items are vital to early success, and which items can be deferred until later when your business is bringing in more cash. You can start with small equipment and then "trade-up" as you grow.

Disadvantages. Many home businesses strangle for lack of space, and they put a heavy strain on the workings of the home-life. Your home's location or facilities may not be suitable. Zoning restrictions may prevent you from operating out of your home. Moving to a bigger, better location can cost money and time. If cheap or used equipment is not selected carefully, it can lead to expensive repairs. Family members may feel "used" if they are asked to work and do not share your dreams and goals.

Advice. Weigh each possibility's benefits against its drawbacks. Visualize working in a home location in all its gory details, including the daily interactions with family members. Check the local zoning restrictions. Select used equipment with care and examine it carefully for damage and wear before buying, and make sure that spare parts are available if needed.

Lease It:

Advantages. You may be able to put off big expenses by leasing equipment or vehicles. This is effective if you need many "big ticket" items to start your business and can't get the needed cash to buy them. Leasing also makes sense if you need an expensive item during start-up, but will be replacing it in a year or two with something else, or if the item is only to be used temporarily. All of the cost of a lease is an operating expense (tax deductible), as opposed to being a part of a loan.

Disadvantages. You will often pay more in the long run by leasing instead of buying. Remember, the leasing companies are making a profit off of you, and that's money out of your pocket and into theirs.

Advice. Use leasing if necessary to avoid draining your cash supply heavily during start-up. Then gradually phase over to buying these items as your profits start coming in. Investigate leasing terms, responsibilities of each party (maintenance, for example), and liabilities (do they insure a leased vehicle or piece of machinery, or do you?).

Rent It:

Advantages. Like leasing, you can avoid plunking down large amounts of cash to buy items which will be used only temporarily. To build your new shop for example, it probably makes more sense to rent a cement mixer, nail gun, and other tools for a short time than it does to buy them, and then find them lying idle and useless when the job is done. All of the rental cost is an operating expense (tax deductible), as opposed to a part of a loan.

Disadvantages. Renting only makes sense for short duration use. Renting costs you money. You may be liable for equipment damage or loss.

Advice. Try to borrow items from friends first. Rent when the duration of use is short and the cost of the item high. Comparison shop, and check all rental terms (suppose you need the tool for an extra week?), obligations (are you responsible for cleaning the equipment after use?) and liabilities (how much will they charge you for damage or loss?). Ask if the rental company will deliver and pick-up the equipment for free, which saves you time and gas.

APPROACHING A LENDER

When the time comes to ask lenders for money, all of your efforts developing a business plan are going to pay off. Here is a checklist of things to think about before you meet with a potential lender:

☐ Determine what the lender wants out of this deal. Some lenders, such as banks, want interest on their money, and want to be sure that you will pay them back on time. Others, such as family, might want to simply help the family as a whole, and don't care as much about profiting off of you. Some lenders, such as partners, might want a piece of the action.

☐ Determine how you will approach this lender and offer him what he wants. For banks, you might emphasize your reliability with the fact that you have had several major auto loans in the past and have paid them all back on time. What supporting documents will he find interesting? If he's interested in high-growth and quick return, how can you satisfy his needs?

☐ Determine if this lender is well matched to your needs. Pre-screen your choices, and eliminate those lenders which have needs which conflict with your own. For example, if Uncle Bob indicated he might loan you $15,000 in return for a piece of the action, you might have to turn him down because he is a crotchety old cuss who would scare customers away. You might also scratch from your list high-yield, quick return lenders, because you need a thirty-year mortgage to buy your new building.

When you go to your loan interview, you should be prepared in several ways. Here is a checklist of things to think about on the day of your interview:

☐ Dress well. Lenders, especially bankers, view your appearance as a reflection of your character. Even if you live your life in mechanic's coveralls and never, ever put on a suit, you should for once make an exception and dress well. It is only for a few hours, and it increases your chances of success.

☐ Collect your documents. Make sure that you have your complete business plan in hand, with all of its supporting material. Run through it one more time, and think about the main points you want to make to the lender.

☐ During the interview, don't be afraid. Banks are an alien environment to most of us, but just remember that it is the business of the lender to make loans.

That's their bread and butter, and they want to make you a loan.

☐ If the lender asks you a question which you are unsure of, say that you are not sure. Don't make up answers, since lenders are very good at spotting thin arguments. The best response you can make is, "I don't know the precise answer to that. Let me find out and get back to you tomorrow." Then follow up.

☐ Take an active role. It is much better to work with the loan officer than to simply sit and wait for him to ask all the questions. Be enthusiastic. After all, this is your dream!

☐ Ask for the loan. Don't hem and haw and walk out. You are there to get a loan, so ask for it. Be direct. "Will you approve the loan for $22,000?"

☐ If you don't get the loan, ask why. Perhaps there is miscommunication which you can immediately rectify. At the very least, it is valuable information to have before you approach another lender. Knowing the reason of your initial failure can help you correct the problem.

☐ If you *do* get the loan, *stop!* It is very important at this point to check the details of the loan to make sure it is in your best interests. If the interest rate is too high, the payback period too short or too long, or other details amiss, you should ask for a modification of the agreement, or even to turn it down. Ask the lender to let you examine the conditions of the loan for a day or two. Take the unsigned agreement to your CPA or financial adviser and have him look it over. If it looks good, take it back and sign it. If there are problems, work on them with the lender. Make sure you don't accept a bad deal.

☐ Be professional about the loan if you are dealing with a friend or relative, and put everything in writing. Even though they are a friend, make sure everything is understood by both parties, written down, and signed. That way, if one party tries to wiggle out of the deal at a later date, the other party has legal recourse.

☐ If you are turned down, keep trying until you get your loan. Be persistent. There are probably dozens of banks in your local area, so keep trying.

USE YOUR BUSINESS PLAN DURING START-UP

Chances are that if you have created a well-thought-out business plan, and have followed the steps in this book, you now have a check in hand from a lender. Now what are you going to do with it.

There is a tendency for some new business toward giddiness once their loan check is in hand. Suddenly faced with a huge sum of money, they think that all their problems are solved and begin spending the money incautiously. Pretty soon they realize that they have squandered the cash which they need to survive for the next year. The results are not pretty.

During the start-up phase you will have many major expenses to cover, and more work to do than time in which to do it. Prioritizing and scheduling purchases and other events will become an almost daily chore for a while. Now is the time to again use your business plan as a tool.

SCHEDULE PURCHASES AND EVENTS

One of the most helpful parts of your plan will be your milestones section. You have so far included only the major business events in your milestones list. Now it is time to flesh out the list with smaller and smaller events until it becomes a useful daily schedule.

First, start with the big events. You probably know the days when your lease begins and when your shop opens for business. Begin filling in other events which need to occur. You need to buy and install equipment, decorate, arrange for inventory, and so on. Write all these events on a piece of paper in the order in which they need to occur. Make sure to leave enough time for each event. Remember, shipments may be a day or two late, holidays may interfere with working hours and with the postal service, and, well, people are people.

Second, flesh out the smaller details. You have three employee interviews coming up, you need to have a sign painted on your display window and you need to shop for an answering machine. Try to get all of the myriad of smaller tasks you need to do down on paper. There will be so much to think about and do during start-up that this list will quickly become very valuable.

Finally, when you get the major details ironed out, place them on a big calendar or in your day-planner book, and fill in the minor events underneath them. You now have a working schedule of things to accomplish from now until you open (and after opening too). Try to follow it! You are now your own boss, with no manager standing behind your shoulder telling you what to do. You have to make the schedule and stick to it.

MEASURE SUCCESS AND CONQUER PROBLEMS

Now that you have a calendar of events, keep daily track of how well you are progressing. Success doesn't begin just when the customer's checks start rolling in. Success begins long before, as you attack and meet all your necessary goals, right from the starting gun.

There are two important reasons for this. The first is obviously so that you can spot troubles and take action to correct them. Corporate weinies, when slowed by a problem, say they are "blocked." When a delivery is late, when remodeling goes haywire, or when something stops your progress, you are blocked. You can spot blockages immediately by examining your calendar. Once you recognize a problem, take immediate action to correct it so that you keep the ball rolling.

The second major reason is that your lenders and investors will be very interested to see how you are handling your start-up tasks. Many small businesses get mired in the logistics of preparing for opening day and are forced to put off that time by days, weeks, and sometimes even months. During this down-time profits are not coming in and money is running out, which both decrease your chances for success and of paying back the loan properly.

Hence lenders want to see specific progress toward your goals during this shaky time.

WHEN DISASTER HITS

No matter how fine a job you have done on your business plan, major problems can hit you. Sudden market changes might reduce your customer base or reduce the amount of money consumers are willing and able to spend. Your predictions of gross income might simply have been off. You might have to close shop for three weeks due to water damage, or you might get sick. To paraphrase a common bumper-sticker, "stuff" happens.

How do you cope with disaster? Some new business owners might simply dive into the problem and try to fix it. Unfortunately, they might also end up spending lots of money on an unworkable solution. Other owners might simply flounder with no plan at all.

The best approach to a major disaster is to sit down with your business plan and rethink your business from the ground up. Logically. By going through the same planning process, you stand a very good chance of making logical decisions which will benefit your company. You will avoid letting perspectives and issues "fall through the cracks." Remember that even after start-up, decisions based on hard facts, no matter how unpleasant, will probably be more effective than decisions based on knee-jerk reactions.

WHEN YOU SUCCEED

Success can do you in. Starting a new business takes more than money. It takes energy and time, and more energy and more time. When faced with one problem after another, it is easy to cave in under the emotional weight of the hassles. More than one new business owner has succeeded in getting funding after a long and vigorous fight, only to become so totally exhausted by the process that he fails to devote enough time and energy to his company.

One good way of overcoming the success blues (or the depression of troubled times) is to take stock in what you have accomplished. Like they say, nothing succeeds like success, so take the time to recognize what you have done. A pat on the back, even from yourself, is well deserved and often sorely needed. By comparing your real-life progress against the milestones in your business plan, you can see just how far you have come. Maybe you have fallen behind a bit, maybe you have had to make compromises. That's okay. You are surviving, and that's an accomplishment worth strutting about! And if you have gotten this far, you can probably surmount future obstacles.

Watch people who are good parents. They use both negative reinforcement and positive reinforcement to steer and motivate their children. Your daily problems (the negative reinforcement) are provided for you by the real-world school of hard knocks. You must often provide the positive reinforcement yourself. There's no shame in looking in the mirror and saying, "I am alive, my business is beginning to show fruit, and I will succeed. Look at what I've done so far."

Not only is this good for your ego, it will give you energy and motivation to continue the struggle instead of being pulled down into the mire of despair. Your drive and determination can pull you through. Nurture them.

When you are succeeding, keep looking to the future. The hiker who looks only at his boots can easily wander from the trail. You should constantly be thinking of new goals and new milestones for the future of your business.

Keep your business plan up-to-date. By checking off the milestones as they are passed, by documenting your new goals, and by recording the progress of the company, you accomplish many things. You gain a record of the growth of the company, which can be extremely valuable when you decide to seek another loan for expansion. Your record will also be important if you decide to sell your business, since it tells the potential buyer where the company has been and what its problems and successes have been. Business plans can rapidly become out of date. You should plan to take a day every six months or so and record the changes and new events in the life of your company. You are its parent, and like any interested parent, you should take regular snap-shots of your child.

DAY-TO-DAY USE: MONITOR PROGRESS

Once you are up and running, and the customer's checks are dropping nicely into your business's bank account, you, like many new owners, may have a tendency to sit back and breathe a big sigh of relief. You have made it.

While a rest-period after start-up can help you regain your sanity, permanent complacency is a real danger to guard against. If you don't provide the company with the amount of attention it needs, profits will drop off, employees will become slack, and neglected items will pile up.

Worse is the possibility that you will be sapped by changing market conditions. The world is a very dynamic place, and about the only constant is that things change. New competitors may move into your area. Old competitors may institute new advertising campaigns targeted directly against you. Or changing consumer whims may make your product rapidly obsolete.

Since complacency is the enemy, frequent examinations of all aspects of your business will be your best friend. To guard against complacency, set regular reviews of your company's performance against the business plan's goals and milestones. Set up the reviews, and stick to them. Every two to three months is a good interval for the first three years. After that, six months is a good interval. Just as it is easy to put off needed chores, it is also even more easy to put off reviewing your progress, since it does not appear to be a critical task.

Don't make this mistake.

SOLVE PROBLEMS

When your business plan reviews do turn up problems, or potential problems, the next step is to take action to solve them. Here again you can use your business plan to chart a profitable course. The technique here is to review the whole plan. Big picture solutions usually work better than solutions based on only one piece of the puzzle.

1. Identify problems.

2. Scope each problem. What is its origin? What are its dimensions? Exactly what pieces of your business does it affect?

3. Examine consequences. Left untreated, what will this problem do to your company?

4. Examine Solutions. You may want to draw on your employees' experience, on your banker, on partners, or on professional legal advice.

5. Examine consequences of solutions. Which one gives the greatest benefits?

Remember that the cheapest solution is not necessarily the best solution. One the other hand, throwing money at a problem doesn't always solve it either. You need to weigh all factors, and plan for the long haul.

INCREASE PRODUCTIVITY

There may come a time when you decide that your business should be making more or wasting less money. Perhaps you see the money draining out too quickly through needless expenses, through lazy employees, or through inefficient procedures. You can use your business plan to help you overcome these obstacles. As above, analyze the problem in its entirety first.

Employees. If you have many employees, their training and on-the-job performance becomes difficult to handle. One way of getting a grip on training is to expand and detail the employee job descriptions in the business plan to turn them into real-life training plans.

Production. You can fine tune your production process by viewing it as a whole. When you created your production-flow diagram for your business plan, you examined each aspect of production, and how these all inter-related. Now use this same diagram along with your accounting books to examine what your costs are at each stage. Then, at each stage, think of ways to reduce cost and waste, and increase productivity, value and profit. By using the production-flow diagram to break the process into small parts, you can examine each part of the process critically by itself, and "tweak" it.

Markets and marketing. They change continually. As a new business owner, you will probably be grappling for a while with the marketing of your product. What methods are most cost efficient? What strategies bring you the most customer dollars for your advertising buck?

REDUCE RISKS

Every business venture has risks. In a changing world, this cannot be avoided. However, you can spot individual risks before they become problems and take action to reduce the likelihood of these risks adversely affecting your business. Professionals call it risk management. It is a three-step process:

1. *Identify your risks.* These could be physical risks, such as the possibility of customers slipping on icy sidewalks, or old and dangerous equipment

which might endanger employees. They could be financial risks — will spending $15,000 on an advertising campaign really bring in more than $15,000 of new business? They could be psychological risks — will you really have the energy to open and run a second store, and maintain both stores well?

2. *Identify a worst-case scenario for each risk.* If a customer slips on the ice, how much could they legally sue you for? If you lose all $15,000 on that advertising campaign, what will your financial state then be?

3. *Implement ways to reduce these risks.* Knowing about risks is not enough. Take action to prevent these risks from occurring. Engineer them out of your business.

How does the business plan mesh with risk management? First of all, it provides a thorough way to examine each part of your business for risks. Second, by documenting your risk management efforts in your business plan, you supply lenders with important "state of the company" information, increasing the likelihood of having future loans accepted. Finally, if you decide to sell your business, it gives the new owner a valuable perspective on the company, its growth and its problems. This information increases the value of your business to him, since he has that much less trial-and-error ahead of him.

MAP FUTURE GOALS

Where are you going to take your business now that it is off the ground? This is an important question. Many small businesses do well their first year, but gradually lose direction and purpose in successive years. Finally they flounder and die.

To prevent this lack of direction, you can map out future goals using your business plan. Your plans might include expansion, a move to a better location, a new product line, and many other possible milestones. Maybe you even want to dedicate the daily management of the business to someone else so that you can spend several months a year in the Bahamas. All these are possible goals. But unless you set these goals as the company's goals, and actively work towards them, they won't happen. You must make them happen.

1. Define specific goals for the next year and broader goals for the next five years. Mentally examine each part of the business individually, and then examine the business as a whole. If you were handed a handful of wishes, what would you change about your business?

2. Run a reality-check against these goals. Are they achievable? Are they profitable? Are they really good for you and/or the business? If not, scrap them.

3. Develop plans to achieve these goals. How will you actually get from where you are now to the goal? What money, energy, skills and other

things will be needed? How long will it take? Are the sacrifices worth the payoff?

4. Document your goals and plans in your business plan, and have a professional review them, much as you did when creating your initial business plan. Make sure that you are not leading yourself and your business over a cliff.

5. Implement the plans. Remember, it won't happen unless you make it happen. On the other hand, this business is yours to command and steer wherever you see fit!

TO SELL YOUR BUSINESS: LEAVING YOUR BUSINESS

There are many reasons why you might someday leave your business. You may see a better opportunity somewhere else, you might retire, or you might have met your personal financial or other goals. Or the business may be consuming too much of your time and energy, it may be failing, or it may simply not be doing as well as you would like. No matter why you decide to leave your business, there are a number of things to think about and do before you clean out your desk drawer.

If your business is failing, have you tried everything you can think of to keep it afloat? Run through the business plan once again, and examine your product, production, markets, marketing, competition and other facets. Have you cut your expenses as much as you possibly can? Are there places to increase profits? Make sure that you have given it a good try before you throw up your hands and call it quits. There are few worse feelings than selling your business, only to have the perfect solution occur to you.

How will you leave your business? There are many options. You can find a buyer and sell them your business. You can hold a going-out-of-business sale to raise money to pay off creditors. (There are many professional agencies who specialize in this.) You can declare Chapter 11 bankruptcy, which offers protection from creditors while you work out a plan to pay them off, while still operating. You can declare Chapter 7 bankruptcy, where you close down and a court sells your assets to bidders to pay off your creditors. Don't however simply walk away — you will cause tremendous hassles for your creditors, your lenders, your landlord and especially for yourself.

When looking at options, try to determine which will give you the most profit or least loss. Even if your business is taking a loss, don't assume that no one will buy it.

Don't be emotionally crushed when you have to sell out. The world is a rapidly changing place, and you often need incredible insight to predict the fluctuations to come. Your drive got you started once, and with the valuable experience you have accumulated for this business, you can do that much better on your next venture. You may be sadder, but you are probably also a lot wiser, and that is valuable.

WHAT BUYERS LOOK FOR

There are a number of things which you will need to demonstrate to a potential buyer to get him interested in your business. Not surprisingly, most of these are issues you have dealt with in your business plan. You will need to revisit these aspects of your plan, and bring them up-to-date.

Predictable Finances. What is the company doing monetarily? If your cash flow is consistent, this is a good sign. A trail of fluctuating profits, major expenses, and unpredictable down-times is bad. Obviously if your company is making money, it will be more attractive than if it is losing money. However, even losing companies can be of value to certain buyers.

Potential for Success. A buyer will want to know what possibilities there are for making the company profitable. Perhaps you have great ideas, but don't have the money and he does. Perhaps he has skills your business has so far lacked. Try to point out specific areas of improvement which he could tackle.

Maximum Assets, Minimum Debts. The more assets you can show, the more your company is worth, both in cash value and the ability to float new loans. Likewise, the fewer existing debts you have, the better.

Product and Production. Do you have a good product, a way of producing it, and a market need for that product? Are your production facilities poor, adequate, or excellent? Is your business plan's production section well-documented to ease the new owner's transition?

Market and Marketing. Do you have an existing customer base? The more regular customers you have, the less the buyer will have to spend on advertising. Can you reach, inform and motivate those customers? How could he improve on your efforts? Try to offer him additional potential. Is your market expanding or shrinking? What drives its growth? What is your market share? What trends influence your market?

His Competition. This is buyer competition. If other companies are interested in buying your business, it makes you more attractive and puts the pressure on him to buy. Thus, having several potential buyers examining you at the same time is a positive thing for you, since you can play them off against each other and raise the stakes.

Risks. How have you minimized the existing risks? The buyer will be just as concerned with risks as you have been, perhaps more so since he doesn't know all the ins and outs of your company. By showing him your risk reduction efforts, even if they were years ago, you decrease his perceived risk.

Management and Employees. Is the management of the company intact, and does it do an effective job? Do you have a trained and competent staff? Or will he have to hire and train new managers and employees?

Value. What is the liquidation value of your company? Book value? Profits? Losses? Cash flow?

PREPARE YOUR BUSINESS PLAN FOR A SALE

Your business plan and your financial books will be your buyer's two main sources of information about your company. From them he will come to a basic understanding of what the business does, and how well it succeeds. From that information, and from interviews with personnel, your lenders, and from his own research, he will determine whether or not to make you an offer.

Since the business plan is the one variable in this equation which you can change easily (changing your financial books is not legal, nor is bribing staff or lenders to give glowing reports), it pays to make sure that it is accurate and up-to-date.

1. *Check your numbers.* Old numbers kill sales fast by building up uncertainty about your reliability in the buyer's mind.

2. *Check your statements.* Make sure that the goal, product, market, and other information are accurate and reflect the current state of affairs both inside your company and in the market place outside. Remember that your buyer will almost certainly be doing his own market research, and will be comparing his findings with yours.

3. *Polish your wording.* Place emphasis on the positive aspects of your company. Decrease emphasis on the negatives, but don't eliminate them entirely. Every company has problems and risks, so be realistic. Emphasize also the opportunities which exist in the company.

4. *Photos.* You are involved now in marketing and selling your business. And as with any marketing effort, there are ways to make it more effective. One way is by including good quality color photographs of your business in action, which emphasize its positive aspects. Continental Catering, for example, might show photos of on-site cooks preparing a flaming dessert in front

of awed guests. Lycra Land could use shots of beautiful models showing off body-wear.

5. *Recommendations*. Likewise, customer, supplier and lender recommendations are valuable. Continental Cuisine could use three well written recommendations from satisfied customers, for example. Make sure that the customers agree to be interviewed by telephone by the potential buyer, since the buyer may want to ask his own questions. Pick your interviewees carefully. If you have a good relationship with your lender, ask him to write a simple, one-page recommendation saying that you have fulfilled your loan contract to the letter. And since supplier relationships can greatly influence the ease of production, you might also include recommendations from them, or at least supply telephone contacts who agree to talk to your buyer to reassure him. Add these recommendations and numbers to your business plan.

6. *Print it*. Finally, have a fresh copy of your business plan printed and bound.

Remember, your buyer may be examining several different companies at the same time. You may very well be competing for his money, also.

CLOSING THE DEAL

Now that you are armed and ready to face potential buyers, you will have to face them across the table and be prepared to discuss the intimate details of your company.

You will probably be asked to give a presentation, and then you will be asked questions about the business.

Initial Presentation

This is very much like your executive summary section of the business plan. Your aim is to give an audience totally unfamiliar with your particular company (but often very familiar with the business in general) an overview of your operations and the current state of the company. Keep it short, sweet, and interesting. Bring samples of your product — Continental Cuisine, for example, might actually host a small lunch for the potential buyers. Use other members of your team to support you, such as the shop manager, your CPA, or your partner (but not the grunts). Use graphics such as flip-charts, slides, even videos (of professional quality) of your operation in action. Remember that buyers, like all other people, respond well to good graphics and to the excitement these generate.

Question and Answer Session

You might be tempted to answer all the questions yourself. However, you can probably make a more convincing presentation by referring financial detail questions to your CPA and operational details to your manager. These are important people to your operation, who may very well be staying with the company, so let them have their say. Your confidence in the team will reflect positively on your operation as a whole, and your buyer will get to meet some of his staff.

Watch Out for Tactics

You can see psychological warfare any day of the week in automobile show rooms. "This is the last Le Behemoth we have, and three other buyers are interested." The tactics used by experienced warriors in the business world can be just as blatant or they can be subtle. Common tactics include pretending a lack of confidence in your business plan or assertions; dragging out negotiations to make you sweat; heavy cross-examining; marginal enthusiasm (on the surface); the time squeeze (now or never, on our terms); and many others. You can use these tactics right back at them, especially if you have other interested buyers. Play them off against each other!

Closing the Deal

After your presentation, ask for what you want. "So, I would like to offer you ownership of the business for $125,000," along with terms. In bargaining, start a bit higher than you think they will accept. They will start lower, and you will, hopefully, meet in the middle at some realistic price which benefits both parties. If one party loses badly, it's not a good deal.

Just as you took your loan offers home to review them, expect your potential buyers to take your business plan home for review. They will research it, interview your staff, examine your facilities in person, and try to verify (or disprove) your claims. Then, some weeks later, they will call you back to the bargaining table and either reject your offer, or make you a counter offer. Don't be disturbed by the slow pace. You certainly would do the same in their place.

Once you both tentatively agree on the terms of the sale, have a lawyer examine the contract. He may be able to spot holes or subtle ways the buyer is trying to rip you off. Only when you are completely sure about the profitability of the deal should you go ahead and sign.

INDEX